HAL•LEONARD

EASY Jazz PLAY-ALONG

Book and CD for C, B♭, E♭
and Bass Clef Instruments

BASIC BLUES

18 Classics
for Beginning Jazz Musicians

T0083894

Recorded by Ric Probst at Tanner Monagle Studio
Piano: Mark Davis
Bass: Tom McGirr
Drums: Dave Bayles

ISBN 978-1-4584-1518-9

HAL•LEONARD®
CORPORATION

7777 W. BLUEMOUND RD. P.O. BOX 13819 MILWAUKEE, WI 53213

Visit Hal Leonard Online at
www.halleonard.com

CONTENTS

TITLE	PAGE NUMBERS			
	C Treble Instruments	B♭ Instruments	E♭ Instruments	C Bass Instruments
All Blues	6	42	78	114
Birk's Works	8	44	80	116
Bloomdido	10	46	82	118
Blue Seven	12	48	84	120
Blue Train (Blue Trane)	14	50	86	122
Blues in the Closet	16	52	88	124
Cousin Mary	18	54	90	126
Every Day I Have the Blues	20	56	92	128
Freddie Freeloader	40	76	112	148
Nostalgia in Times Square	22	58	94	130
Now See How You Are	24	60	96	132
Now's the Time	26	62	98	134
The Sermon	28	64	100	136
Sonnymoon for Two	30	66	102	138
Tenor Madness	32	68	104	140
Things Ain't What They Used to Be	34	70	106	142
Turnaround	36	72	108	144
Two Degrees East, Three Degrees West	38	74	110	146

BOOK

CONTENTS

TITLE	CD Track Number
All Blues	1
Birk's Works	2
Bloomdido	3
Blue Seven	4
Blue Train (Blue Trane)	5
Blues in the Closet	6
Cousin Mary	7
Every Day I Have the Blues	8
Freddie Freeloader	9
Nostalgia in Times Square	10
Now See How You Are	11
Now's the Time	12
The Sermon	13
Sonnymoon for Two	14
Tenor Madness	15
Things Ain't What They Used to Be	16
Turnaround	17
Two Degrees East, Three Degrees West	18
B♭ Tuning Notes	19

CD

ALL BLUES

C VERSION

BY MILES DAVIS

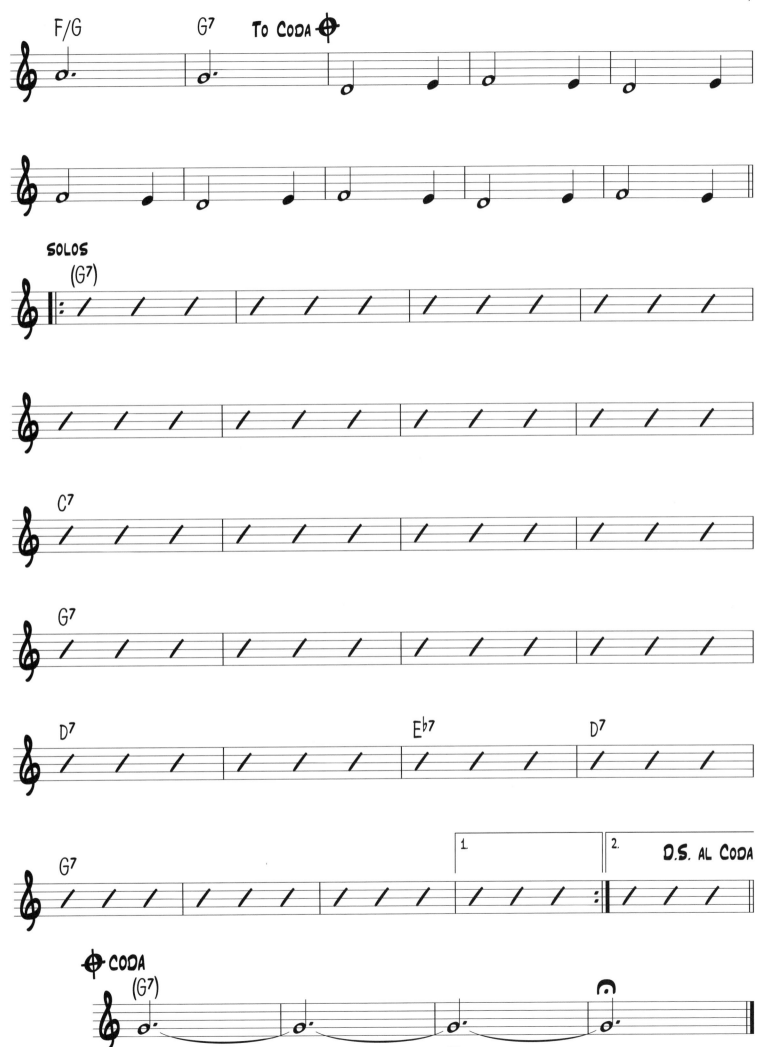

BIRK'S WORKS

C VERSION

BY DIZZY GILLESPIE

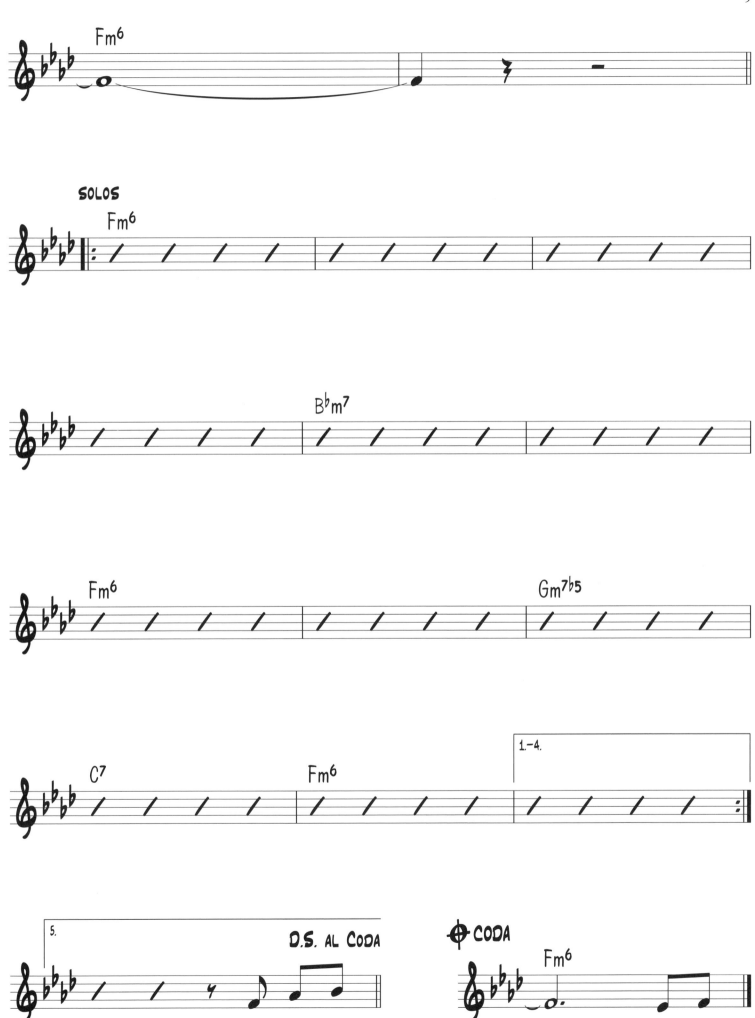

BLOOMDIDO

C VERSION

BY CHARLIE PARKER

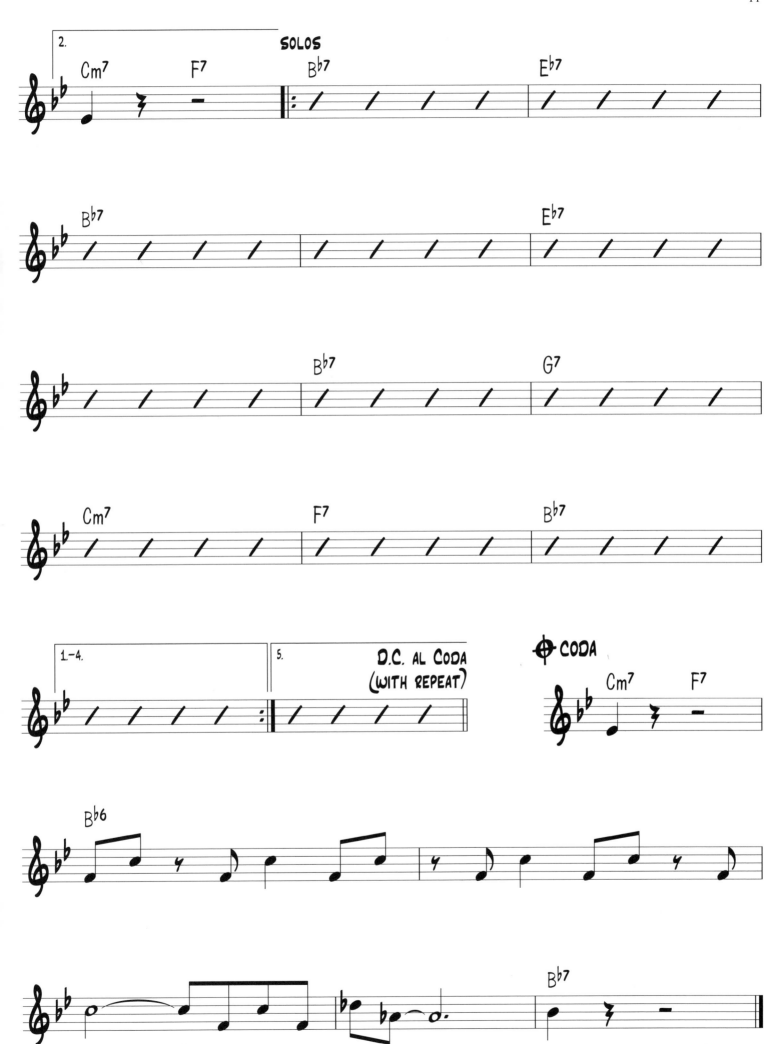

BLUE SEVEN

C VERSION

BY SONNY ROLLINS

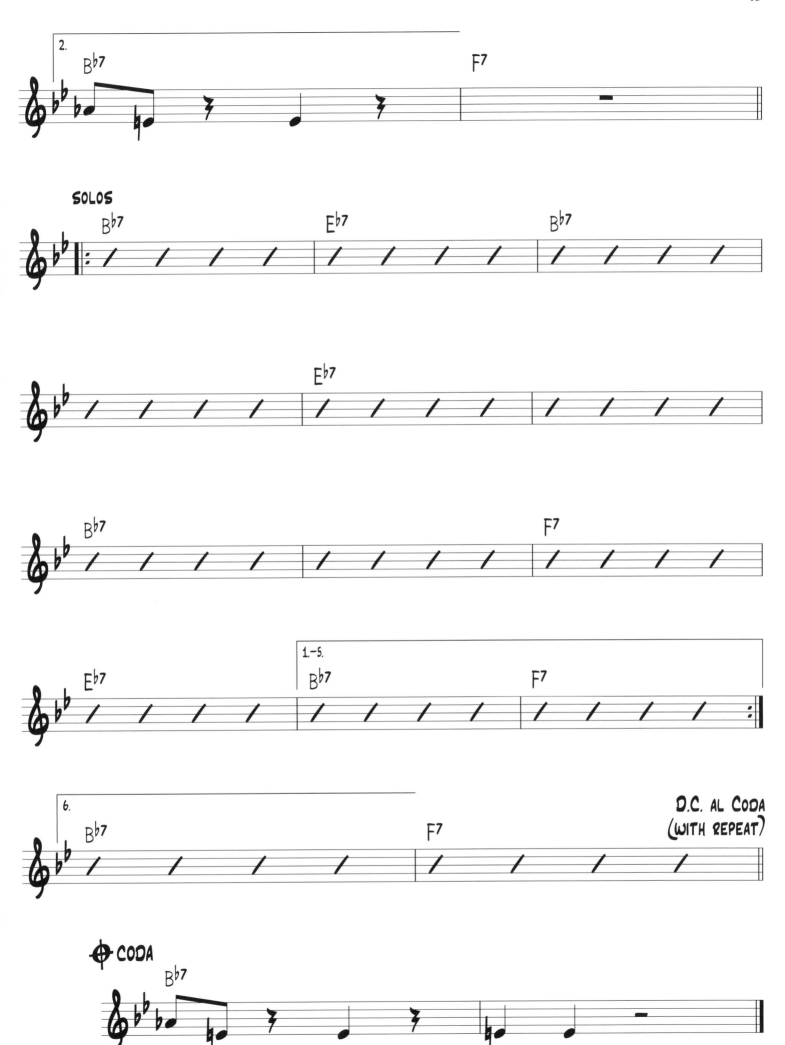

BLUE TRAIN
(Blue Trane)

C VERSION

BY JOHN COLTRANE

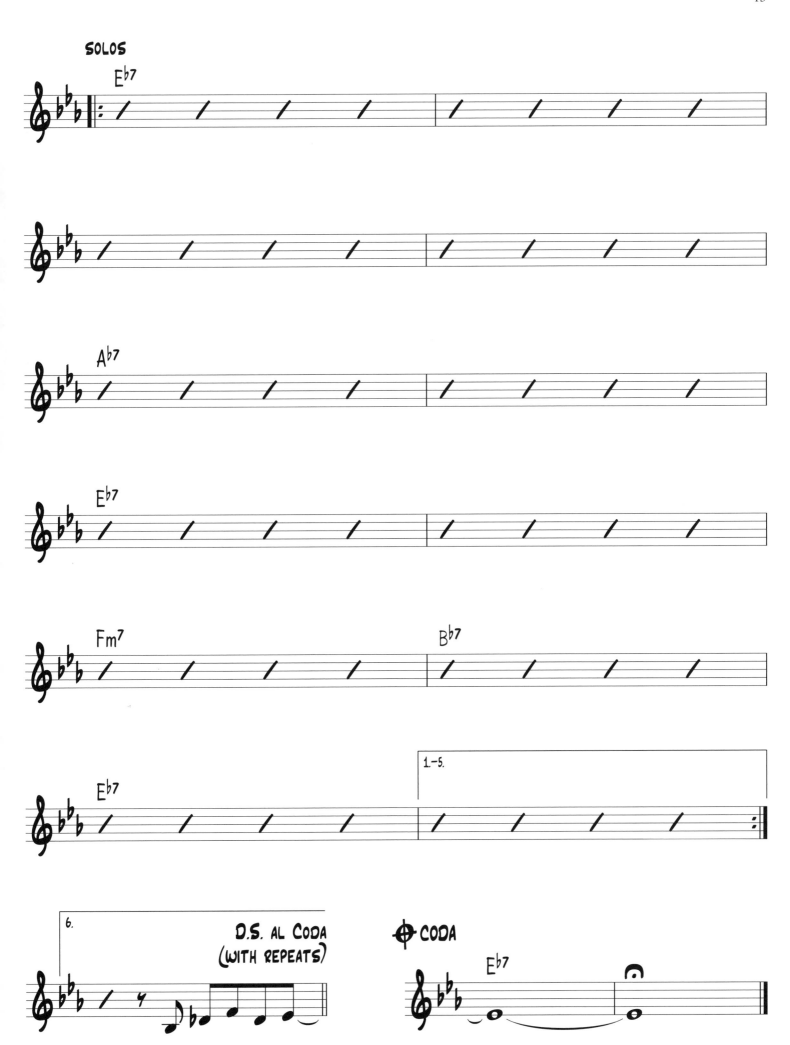

Blues in the Closet

C Version

By Oscar Pettiford

COUSIN MARY

C VERSION

BY JOHN COLTRANE

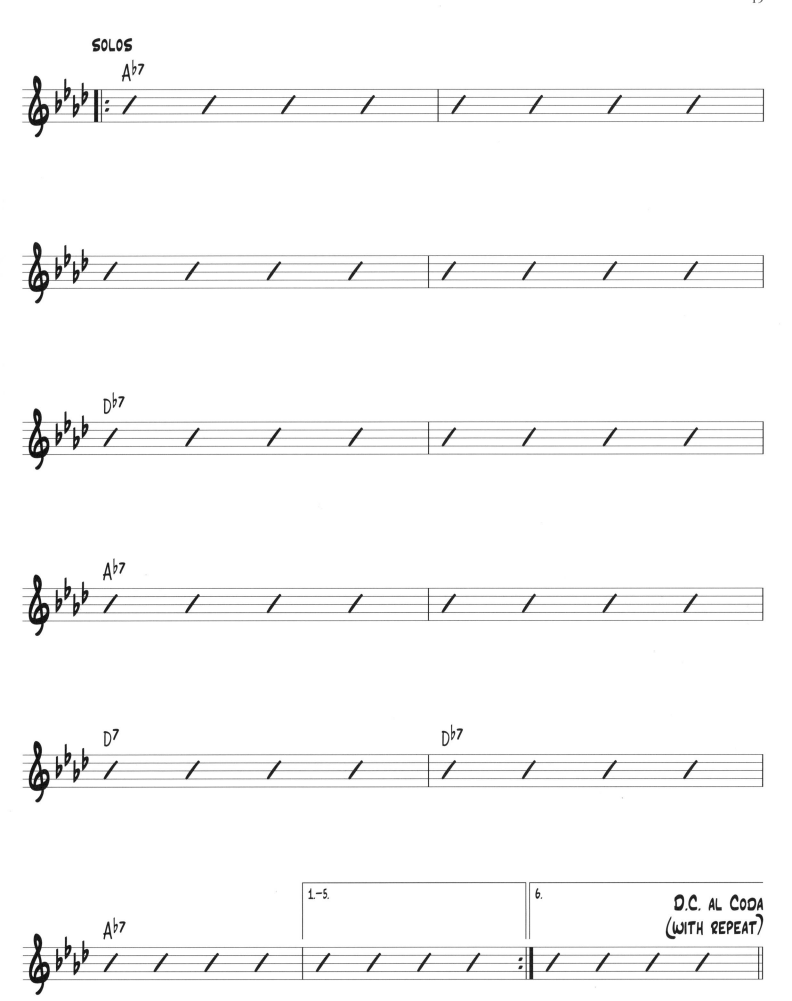

Every Day I Have the Blues

C Version

Words and Music by
Peter Chatman

Nostalgia in Times Square

C Version

By Charles Mingus

Now See How You Are

C Version

By Oscar Pettiford
and Woody Harris

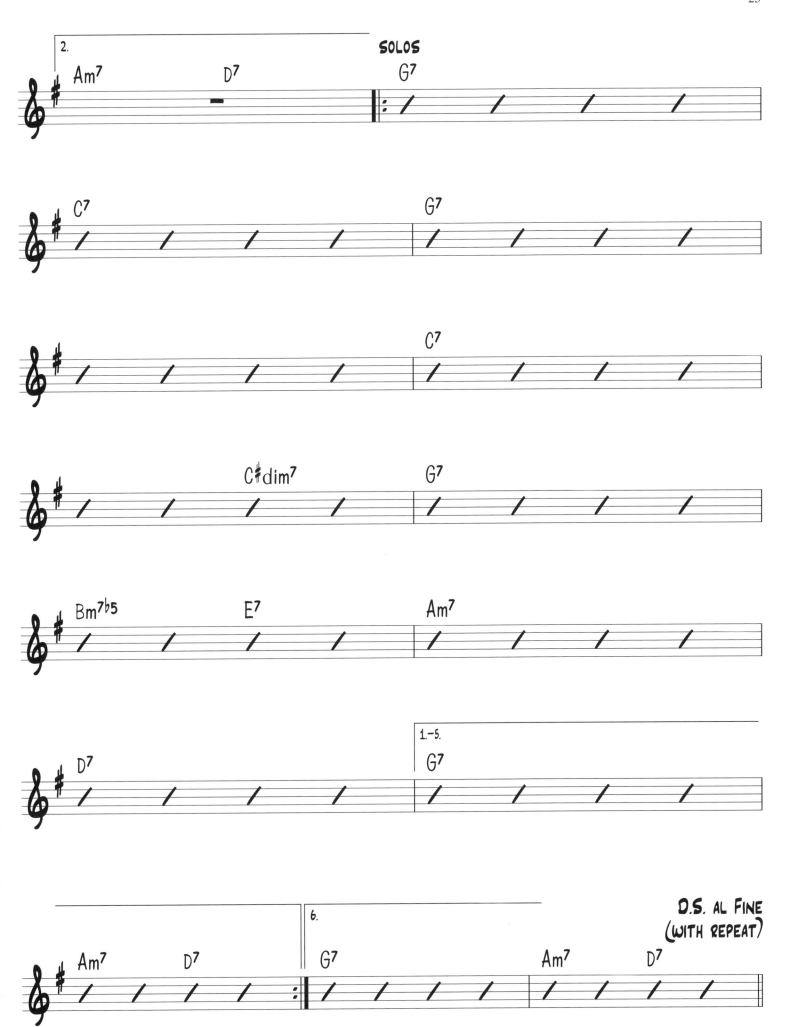

Now's the Time

C Version

BY CHARLIE PARKER

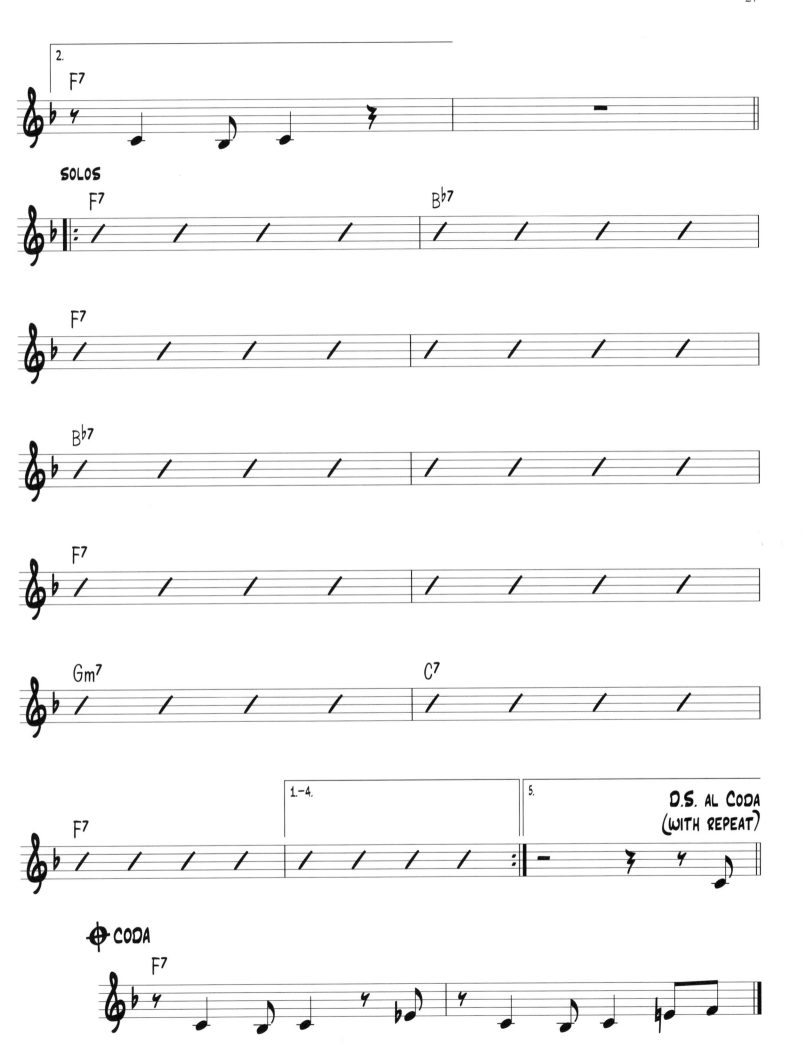

THE SERMON

C VERSION

BY HAMPTON HAWES

Sonnymoon for Two

C Version

By Sonny Rollins

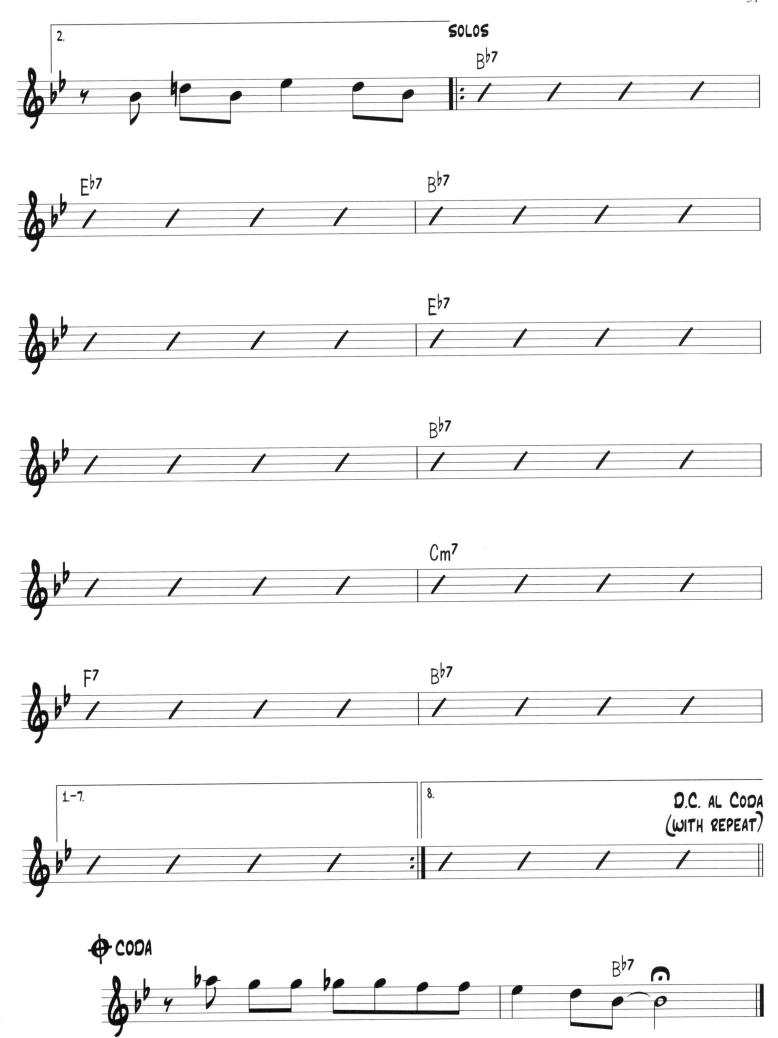

TENOR MADNESS

C VERSION

BY SONNY ROLLINS

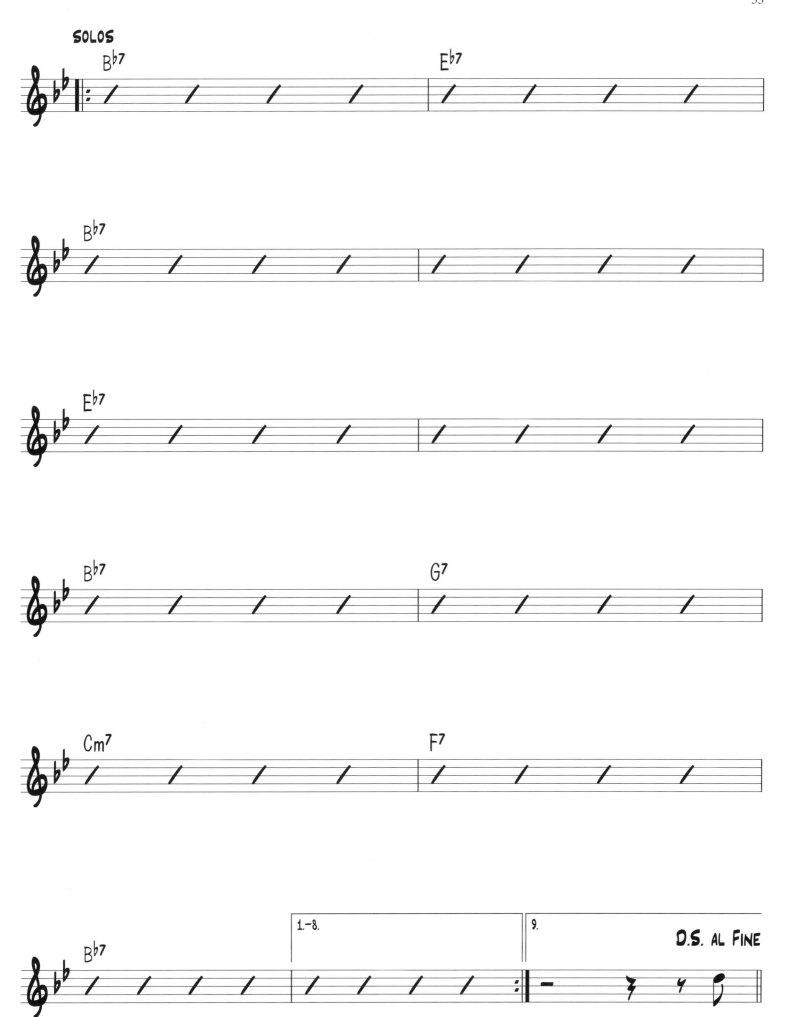

THINGS AIN'T WHAT THEY USED TO BE

C VERSION

BY MERCER ELLINGTON

35

Turnaround

C VERSION

BY ORNETTE COLEMAN

Two Degrees East, Three Degrees West

C Version

By John Lewis

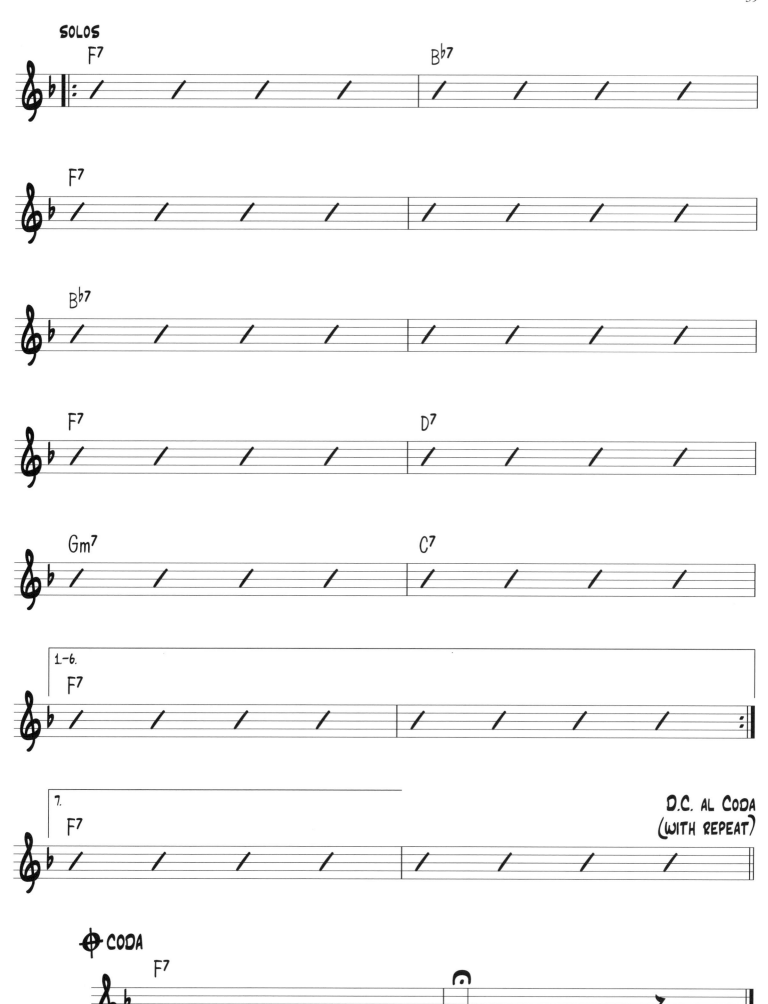

FREDDIE FREELOADER

C VERSION

BY MILES DAVIS

B♭ INSTRUMENTS

ALL BLUES

BY MILES DAVIS

Bb VERSION

BIRK'S WORKS

BY DIZZY GILLESPIE

Bb VERSION

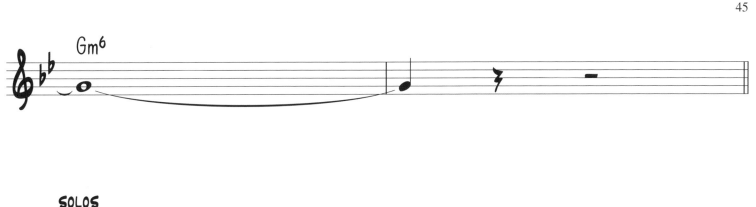

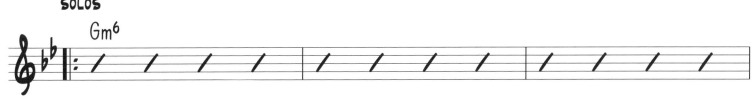

BLOOMDIDO

BY CHARLIE PARKER

Bb VERSION

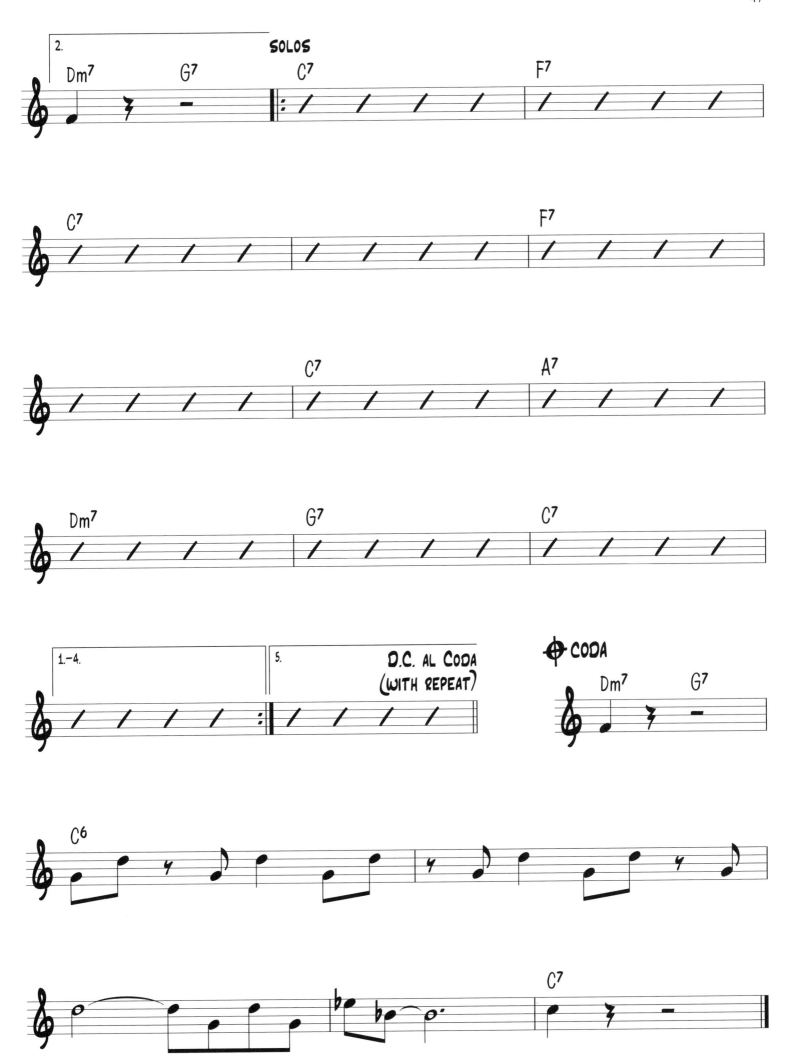

Blue Seven

Bb Version

By Sonny Rollins

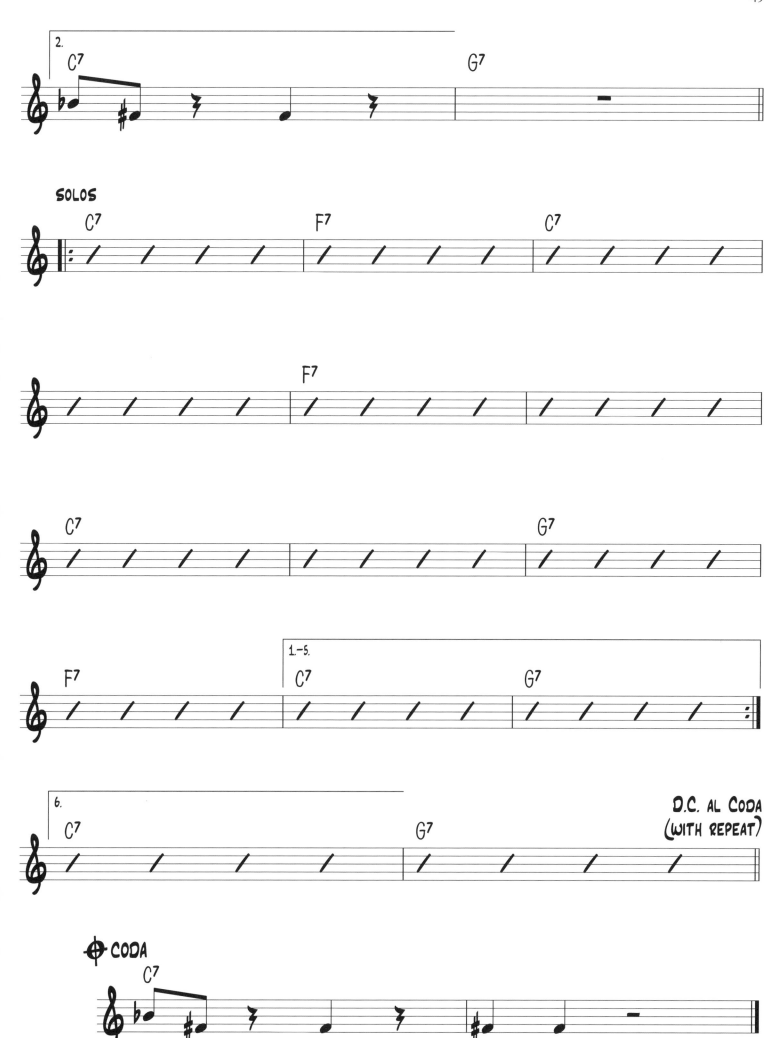

BLUE TRAIN
(BLUE TRANE)

BY JOHN COLTRANE

Bb VERSION

SOLOS

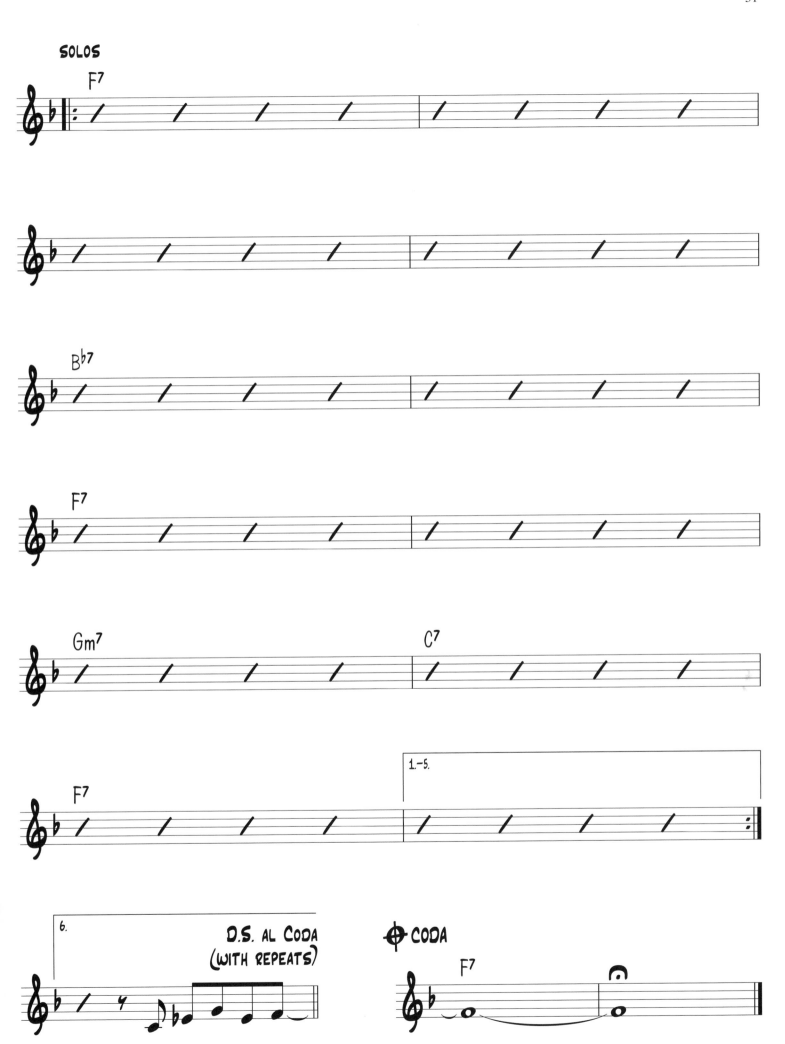

BLUES IN THE CLOSET

Bb VERSION

BY OSCAR PETTIFORD

Cousin Mary

By John Coltrane

Bb Version

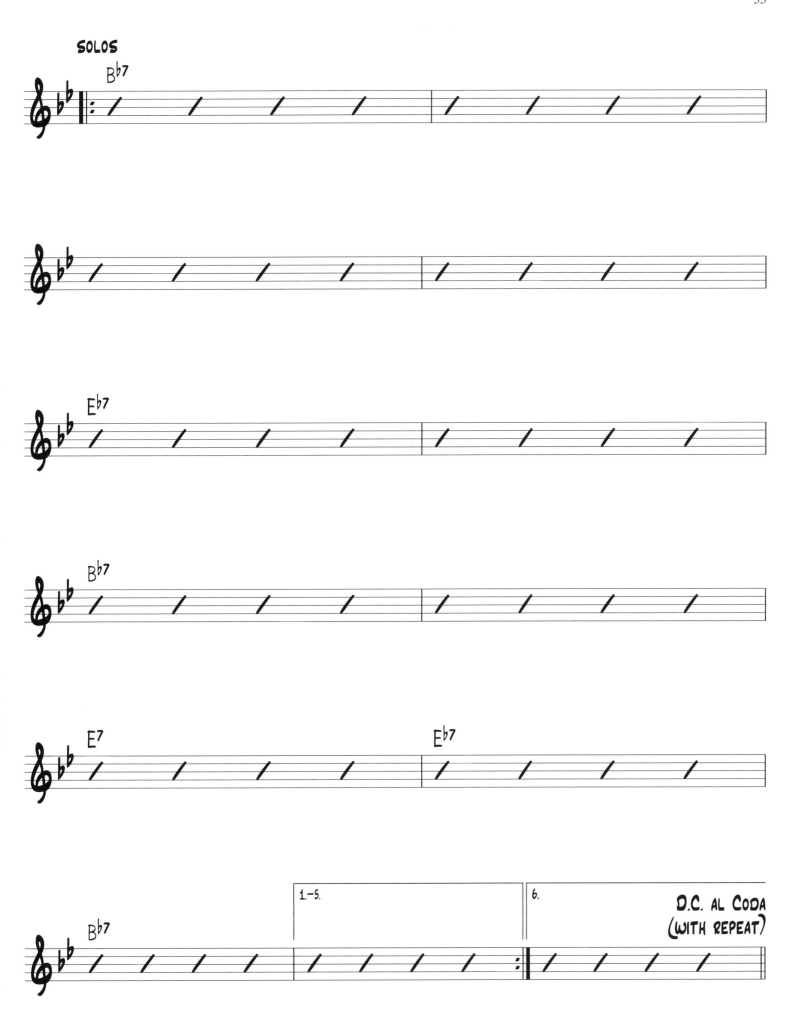

Every Day I Have the Blues

Bb Version

Words and Music by
Peter Chatman

Medium Shuffle

Nostalgia in Times Square

By Charles Mingus

Bb Version

SOLOS

Now See How You Are

By Oscar Pettiford
and Woody Harris

8b Version

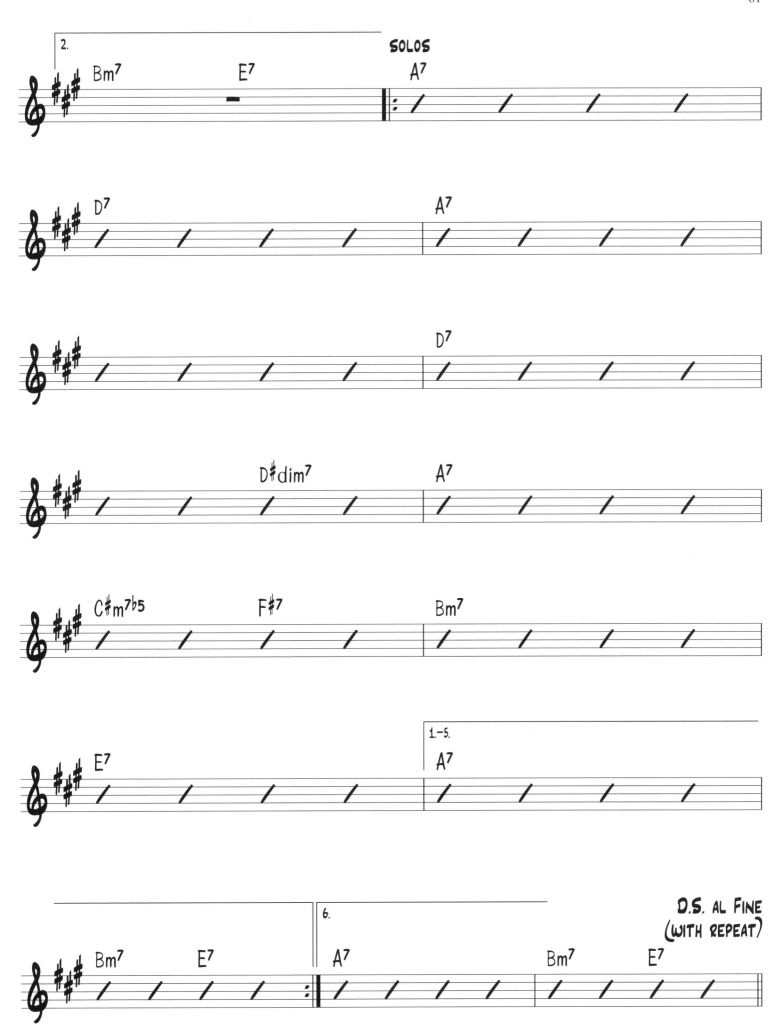

Now's the Time

By Charlie Parker

Bb Version

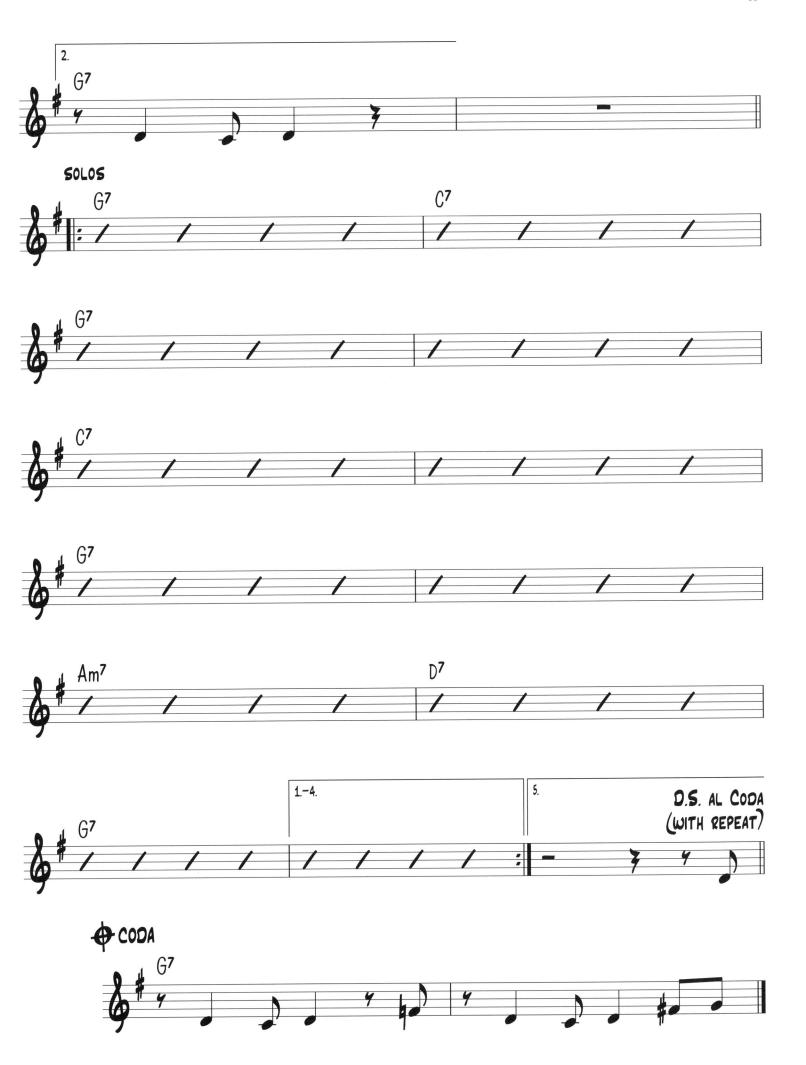

THE SERMON

BY HAMPTON HAWES

Bb Version

65

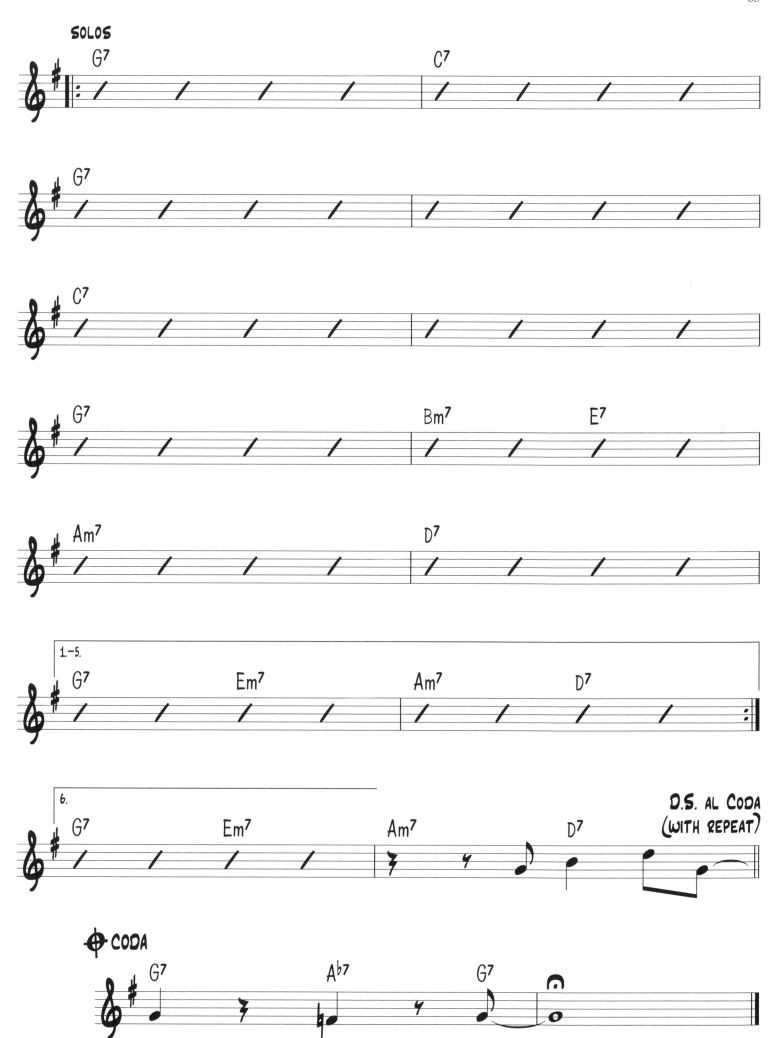

Sonnymoon for Two

By Sonny Rollins

Bb Version

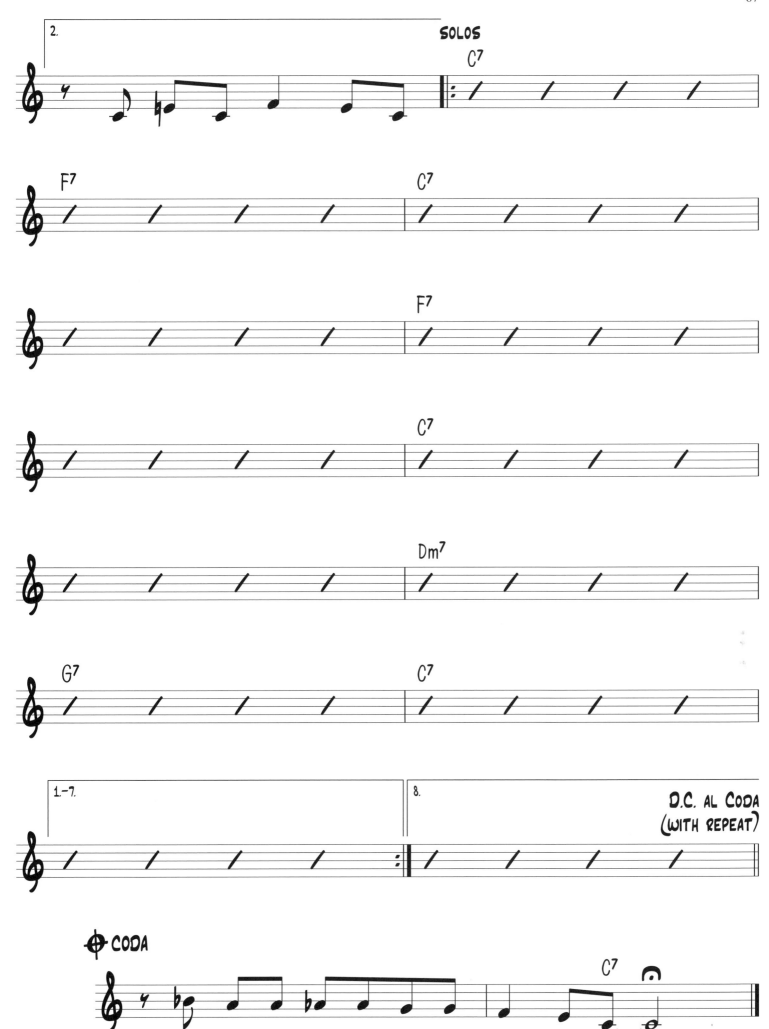

TENOR MADNESS

BY SONNY ROLLINS

Bb VERSION

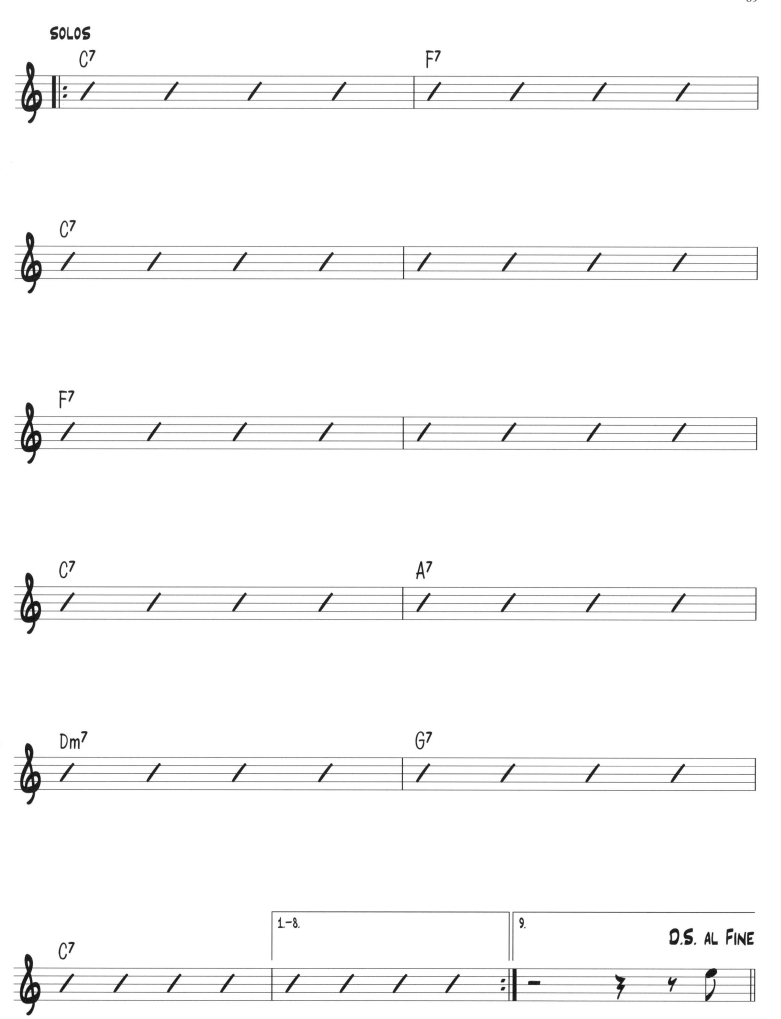

Things Ain't What They Used to Be

By Mercer Ellington

Bb Version

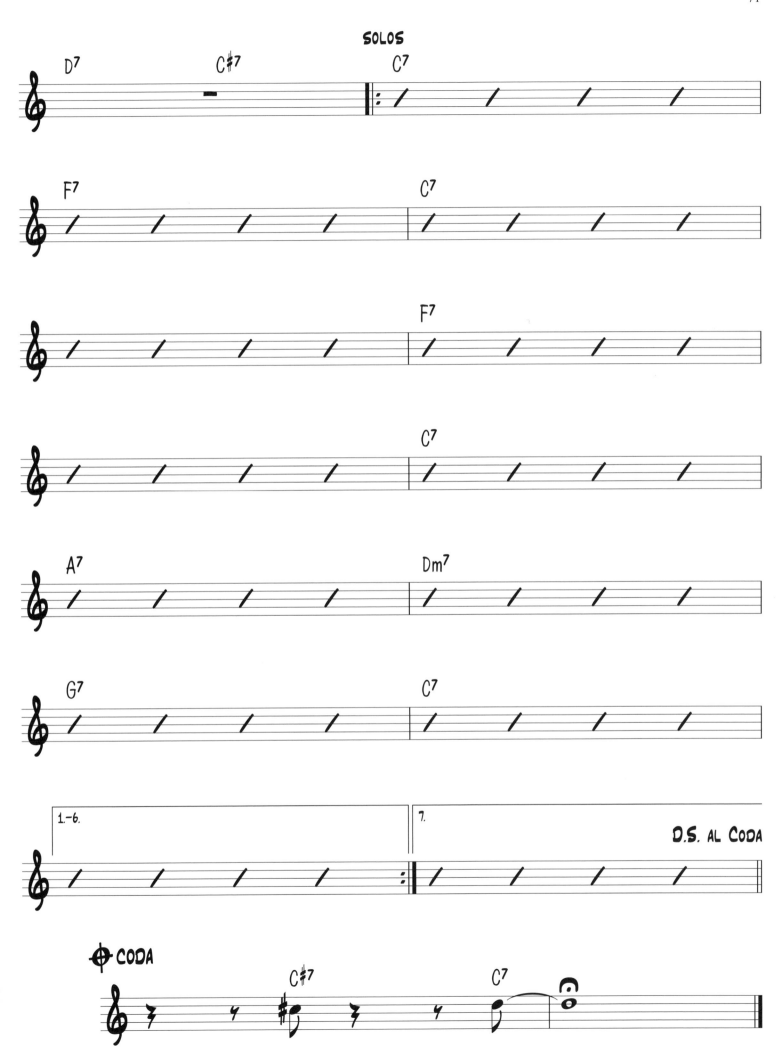

Turnaround

BY ORNETTE COLEMAN

Bb VERSION

Two Degrees East, Three Degrees West

By John Lewis

Bb Version

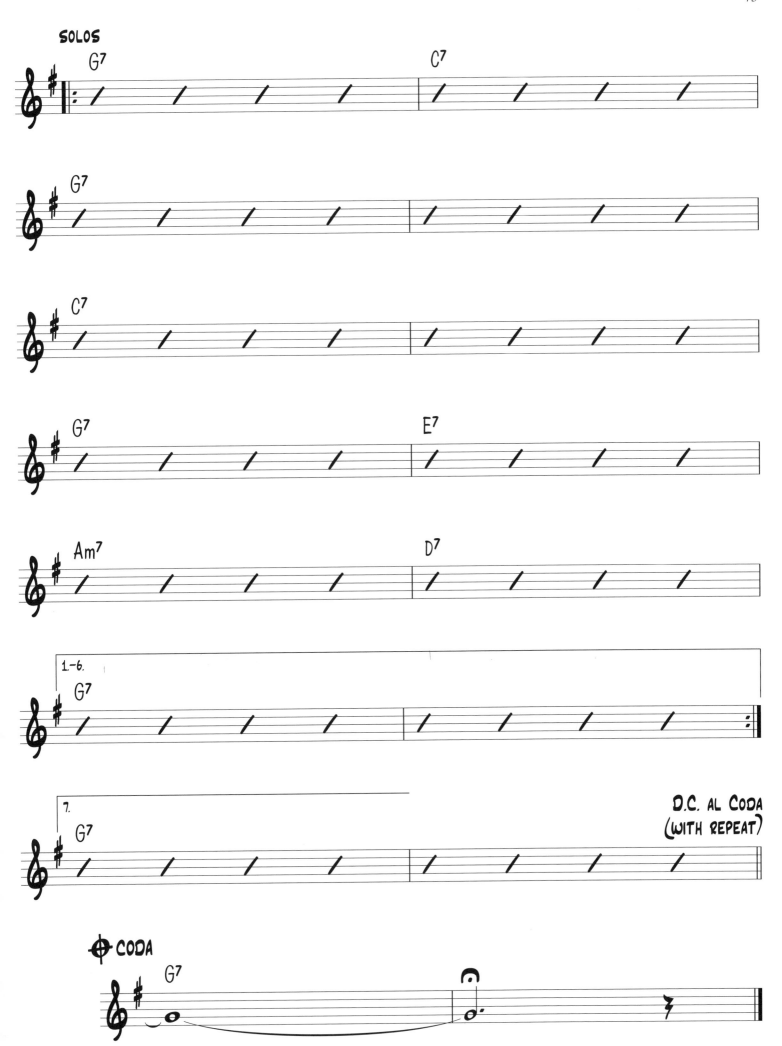

FREDDIE FREELOADER

BY MILES DAVIS

Bb VERSION

E♭ Instruments

ALL BLUES

BY MILES DAVIS

Eb Version

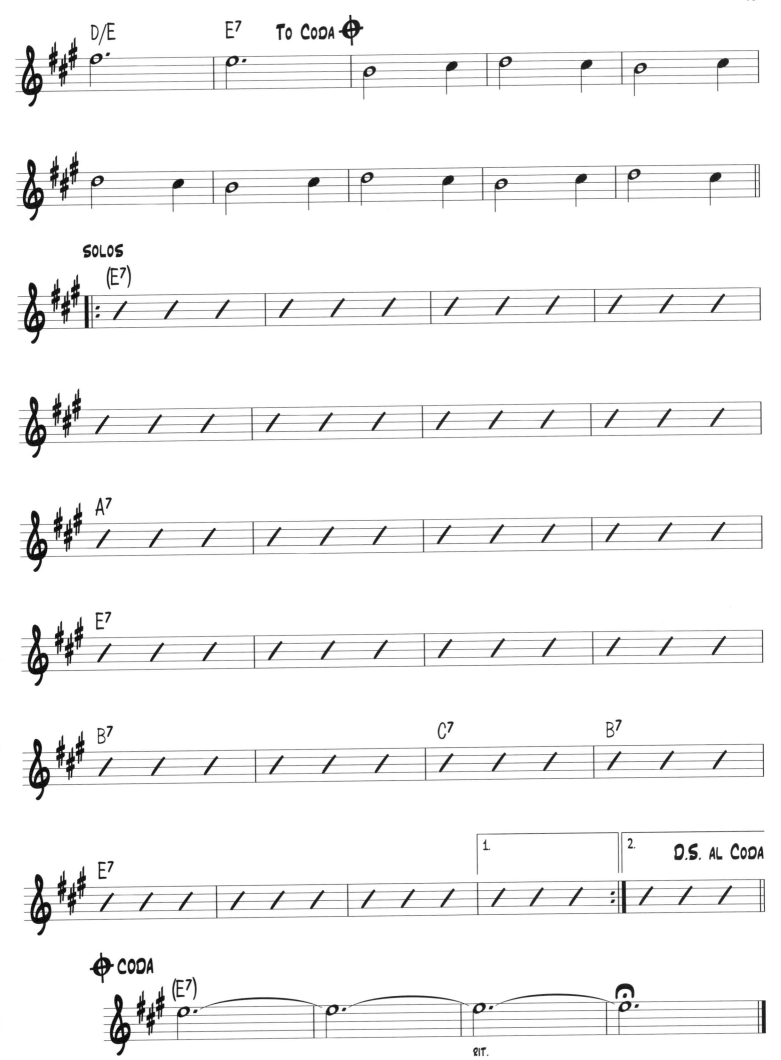

BIRK'S WORKS

BY DIZZY GILLESPIE

Eb VERSION

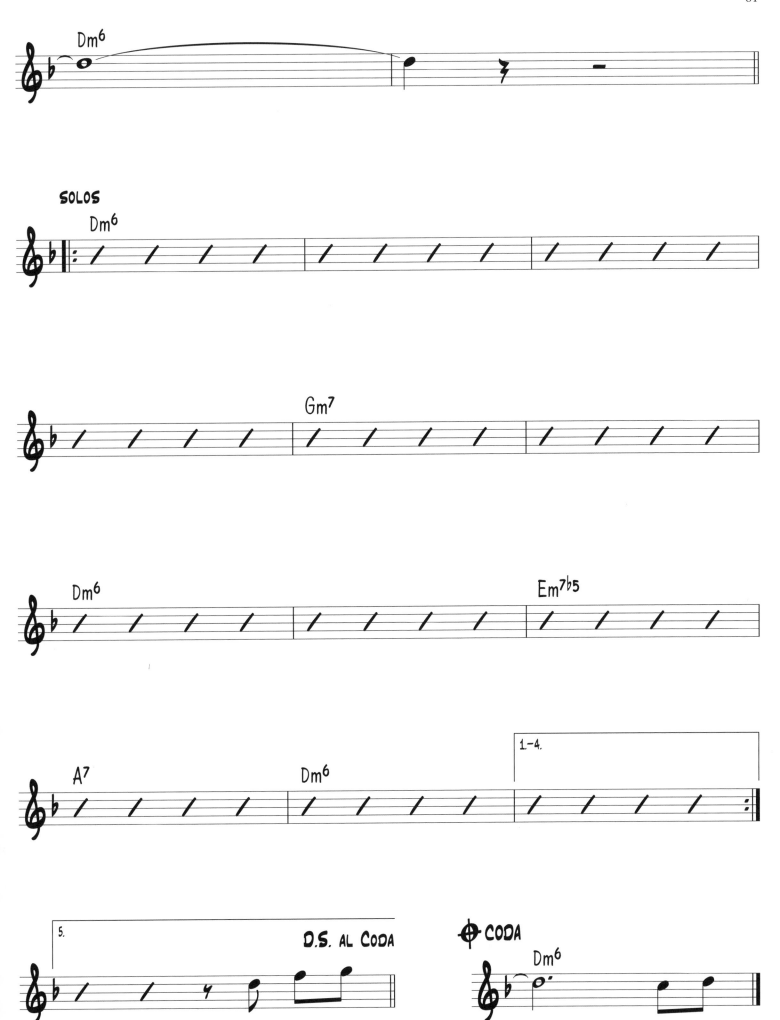

BLOOMDIDO

BY CHARLIE PARKER

Eb Version

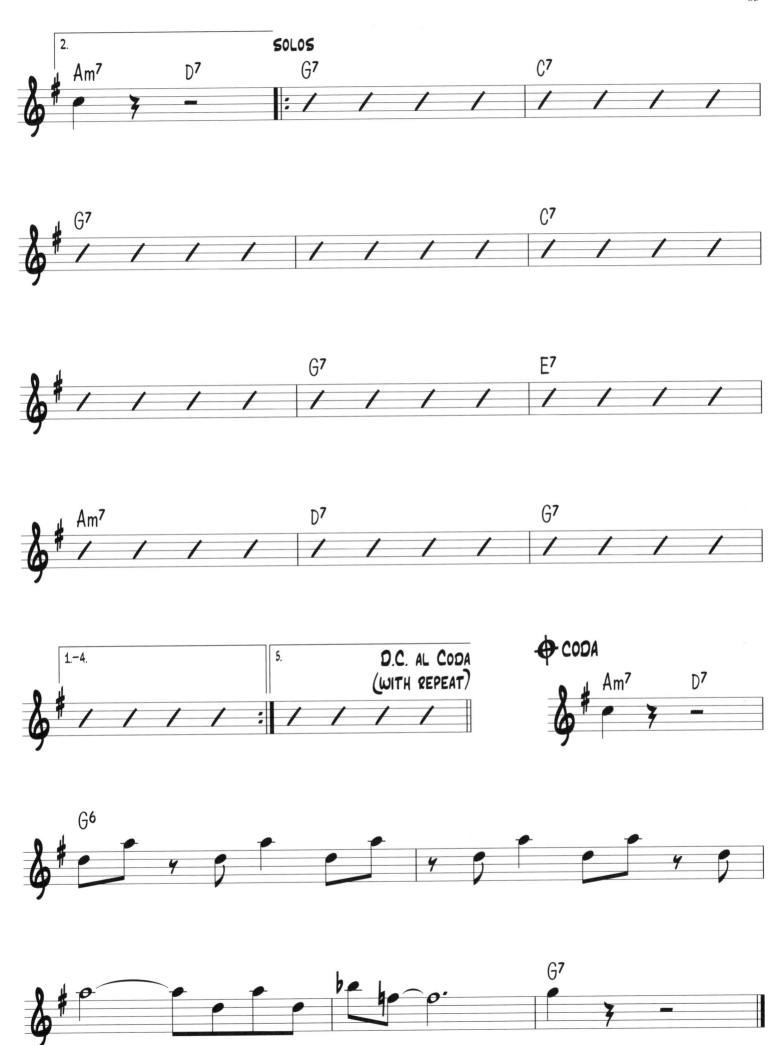

BLUE SEVEN

BY SONNY ROLLINS

Eb VERSION

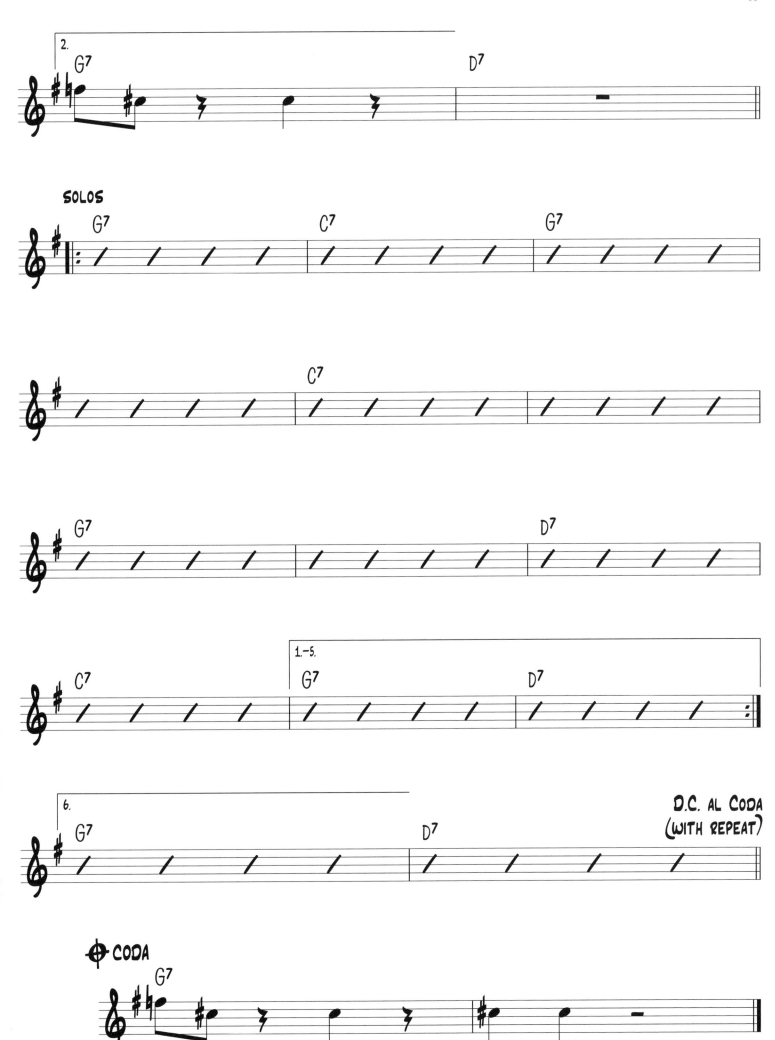

BLUE TRAIN
(BLUE TRANE)

BY JOHN COLTRANE

Eb VERSION

BLUES IN THE CLOSET

Eb VERSION

BY OSCAR PETTIFORD

Cousin Mary

By John Coltrane

Eb Version

SOLOS

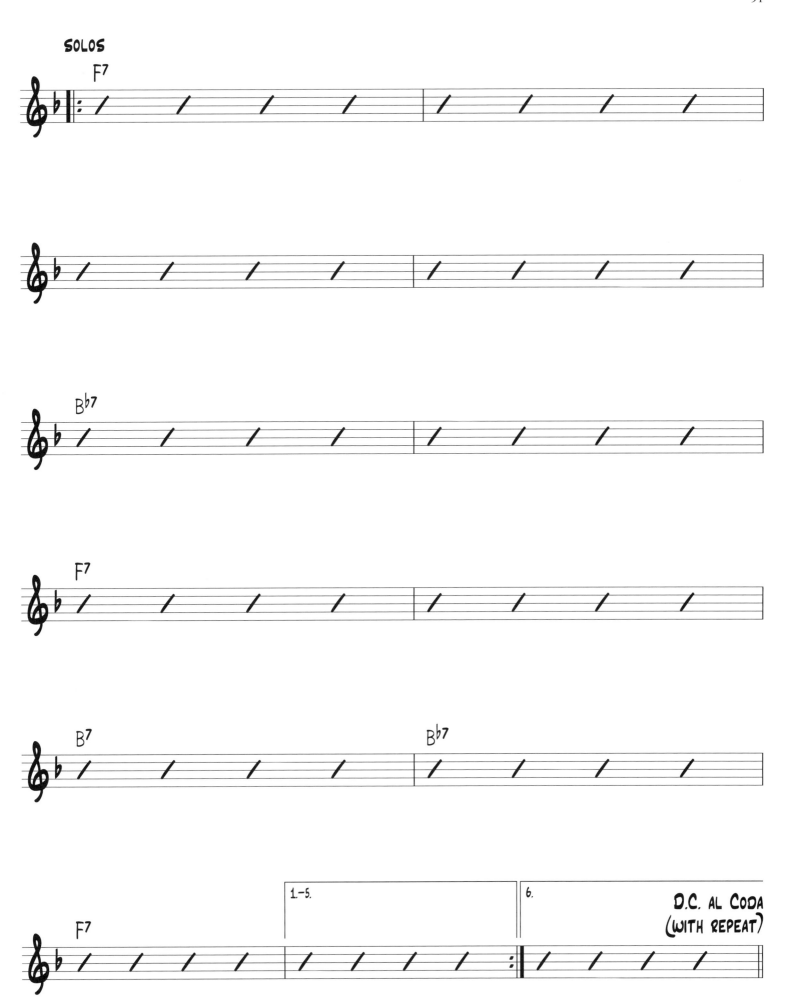

Every Day I Have the Blues

Words and Music by
Peter Chatman

Eb Version

Nostalgia in Times Square

Eb Version

By Charles Mingus

Now See How You Are

Eb Version

By Oscar Pettiford
and Woody Harris

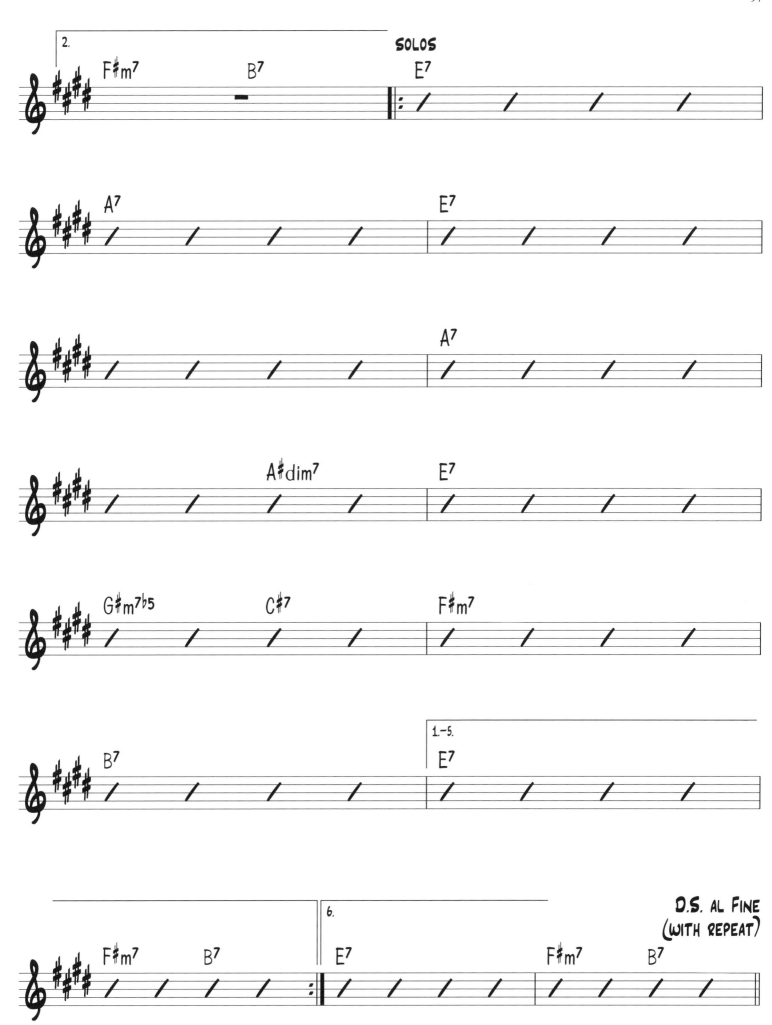

NOW'S THE TIME

BY CHARLIE PARKER

Eb Version

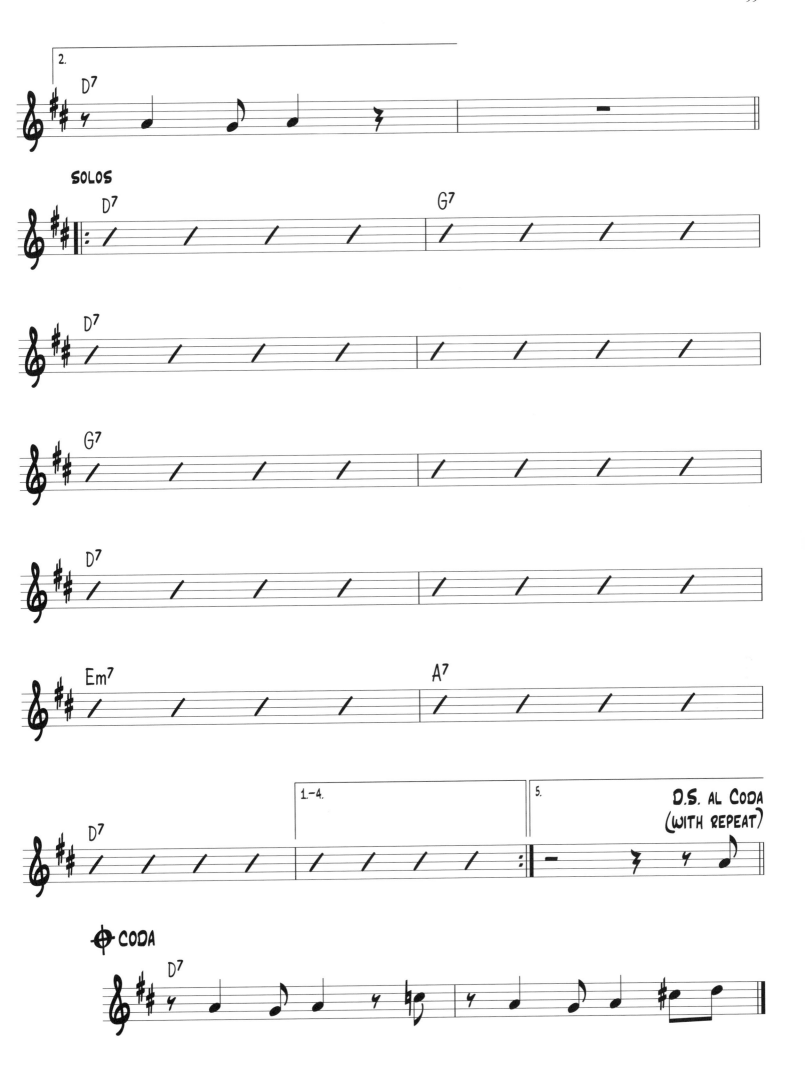

THE SERMON

BY HAMPTON HAWES

Eb VERSION

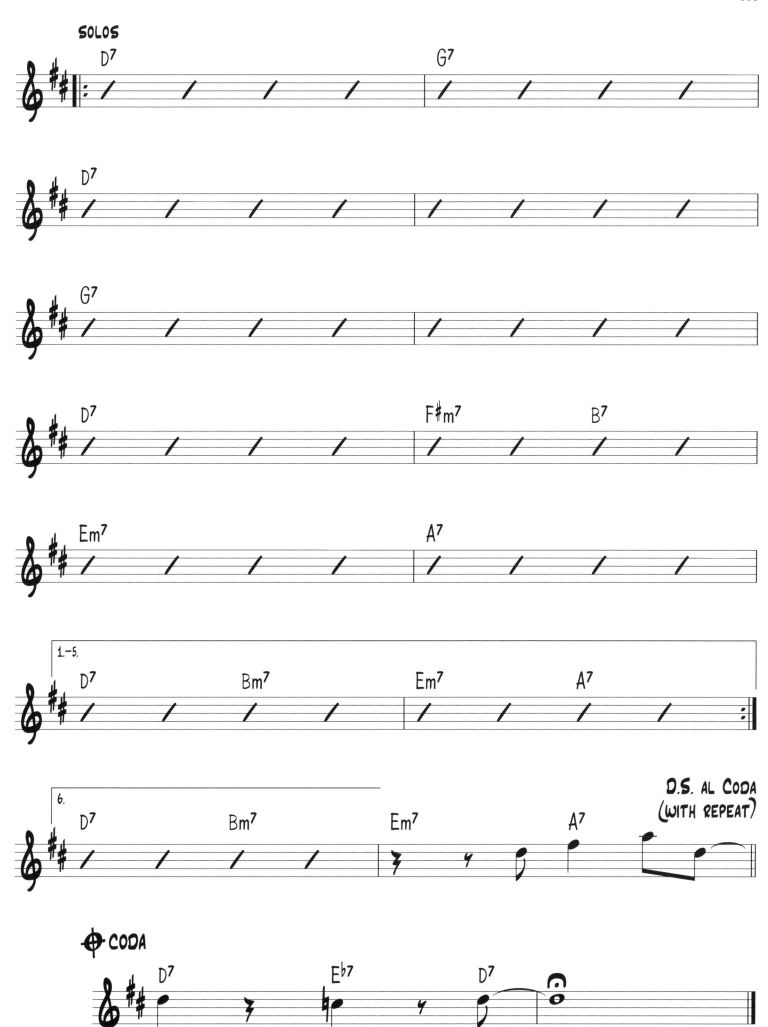

Sonnymoon for Two

By Sonny Rollins

Eb Version

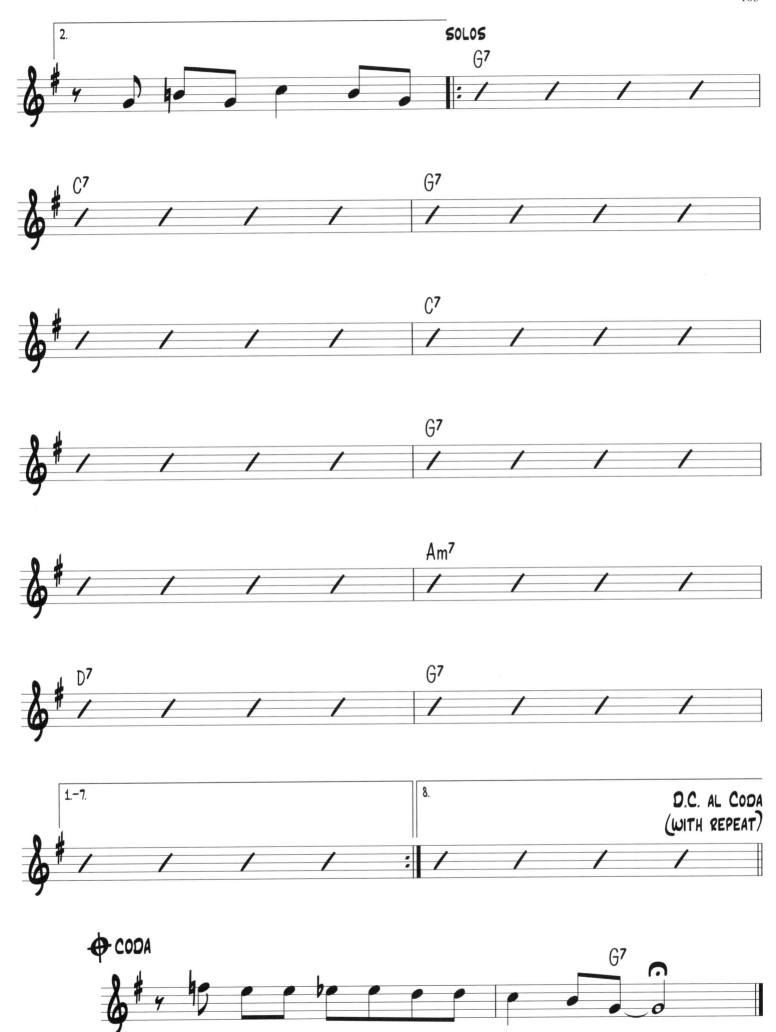

Tenor Madness

Eb Version

BY SONNY ROLLINS

Things Ain't What They Used to Be

BY MERCER ELLINGTON

Eb Version

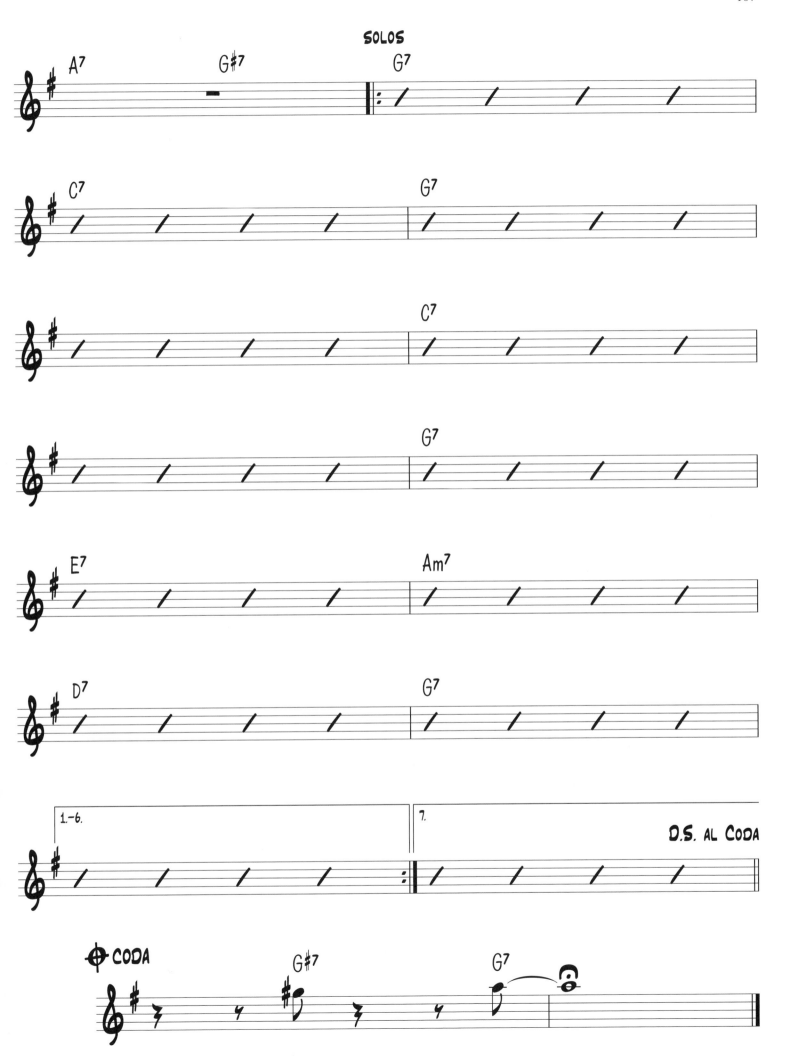

Turnaround

BY ORNETTE COLEMAN

Eb VERSION

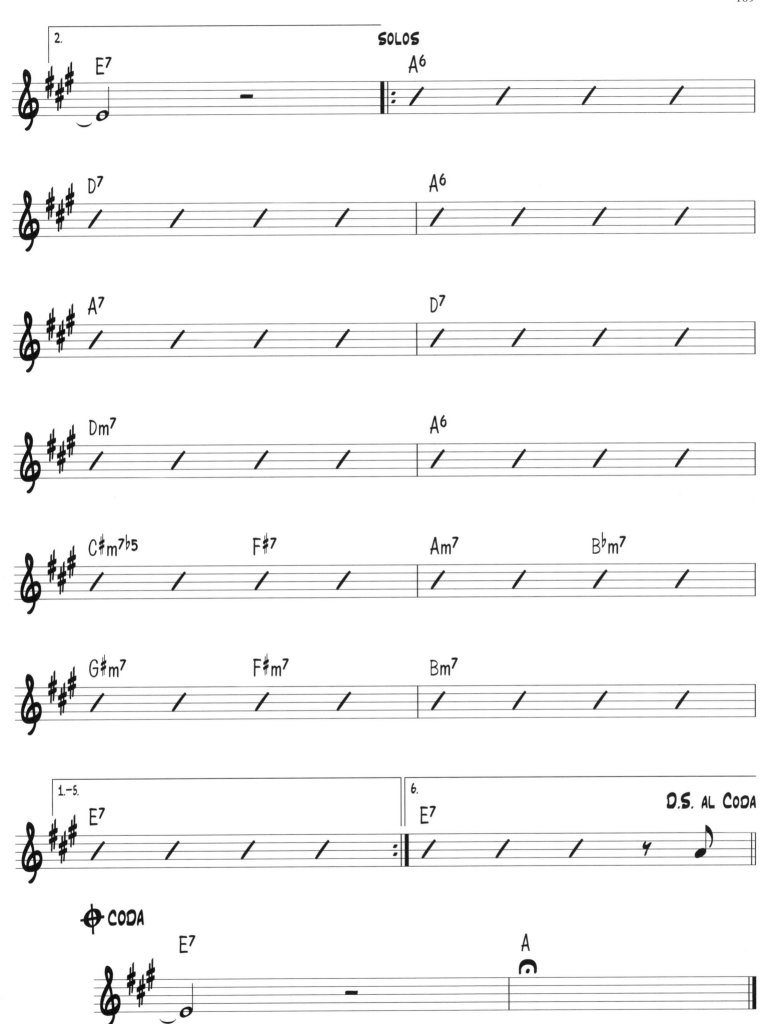

Two Degrees East, Three Degrees West

By John Lewis

Eb Version

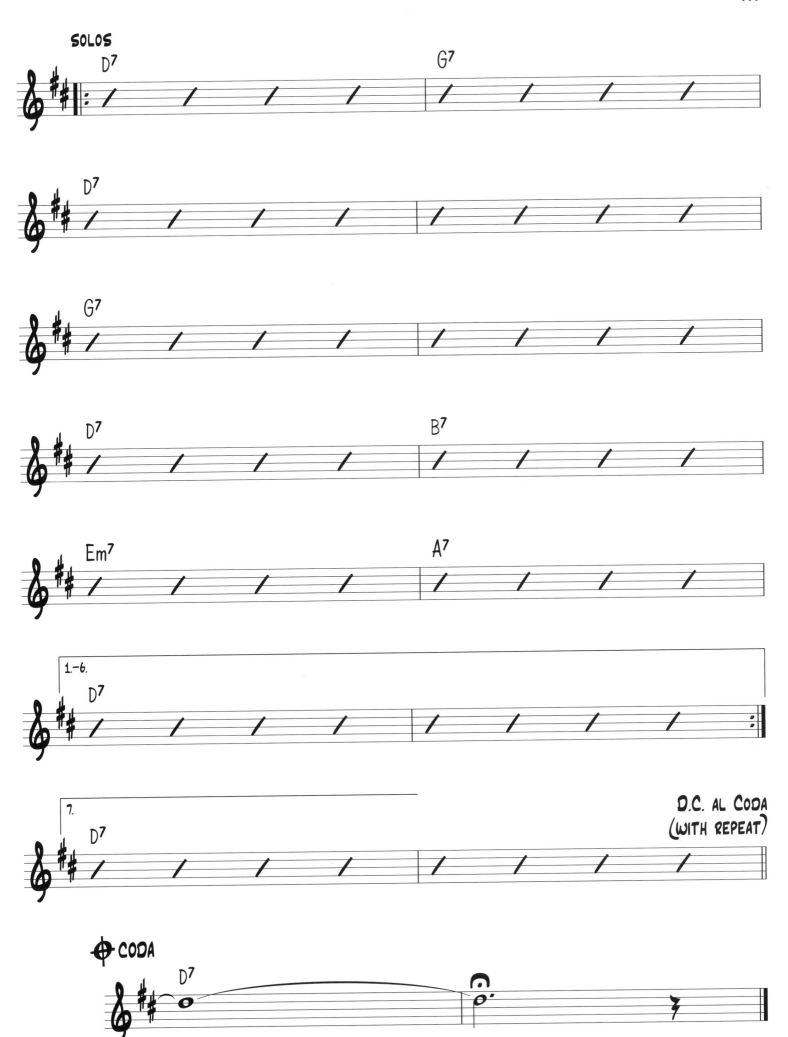

FREDDIE FREELOADER

Eb VERSION

BY MILES DAVIS

C BASS INSTRUMENTS

ALL BLUES

By Miles Davis

9: C Version

BIRK'S WORKS

𝄢 C VERSION

BY DIZZY GILLESPIE

BLOOMDIDO

C Version

BY CHARLIE PARKER

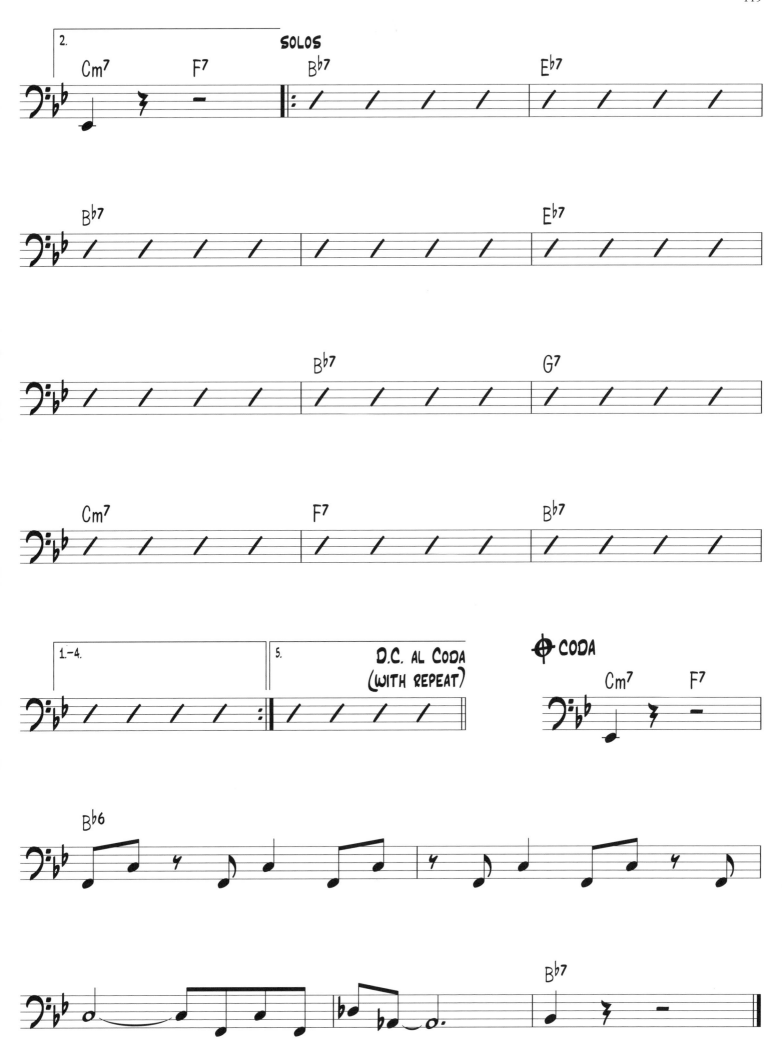

Blue Seven

𝄢 C Version

By Sonny Rollins

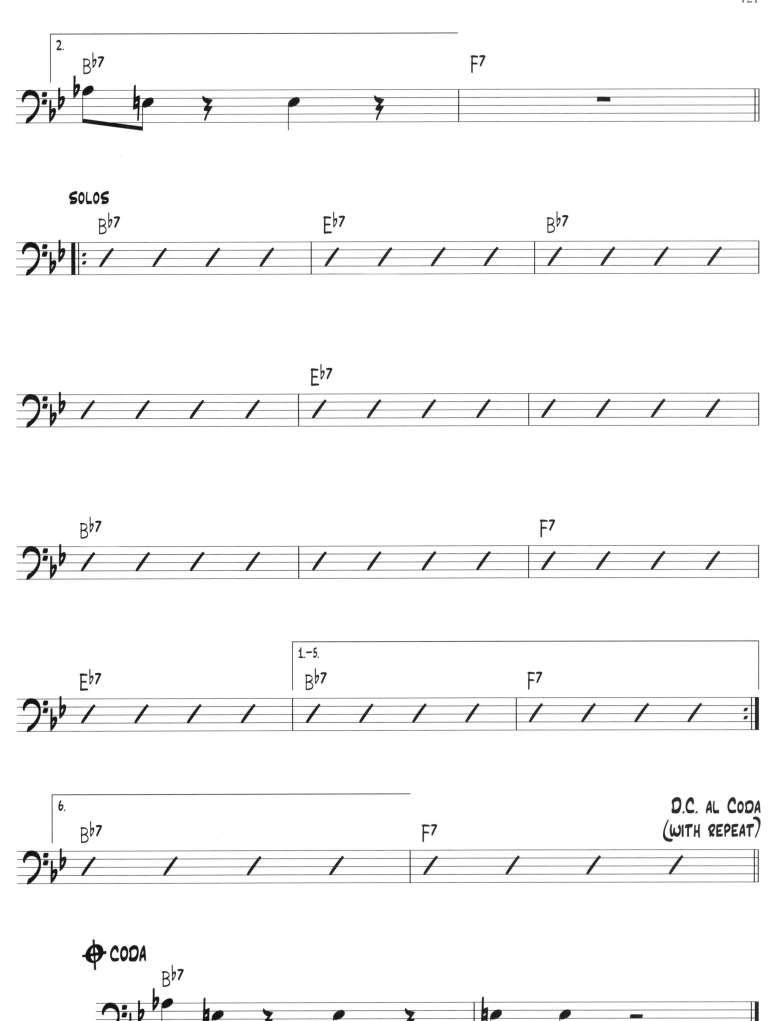

BLUE TRAIN
(Blue Trane)

BY JOHN COLTRANE

𝄢 C VERSION

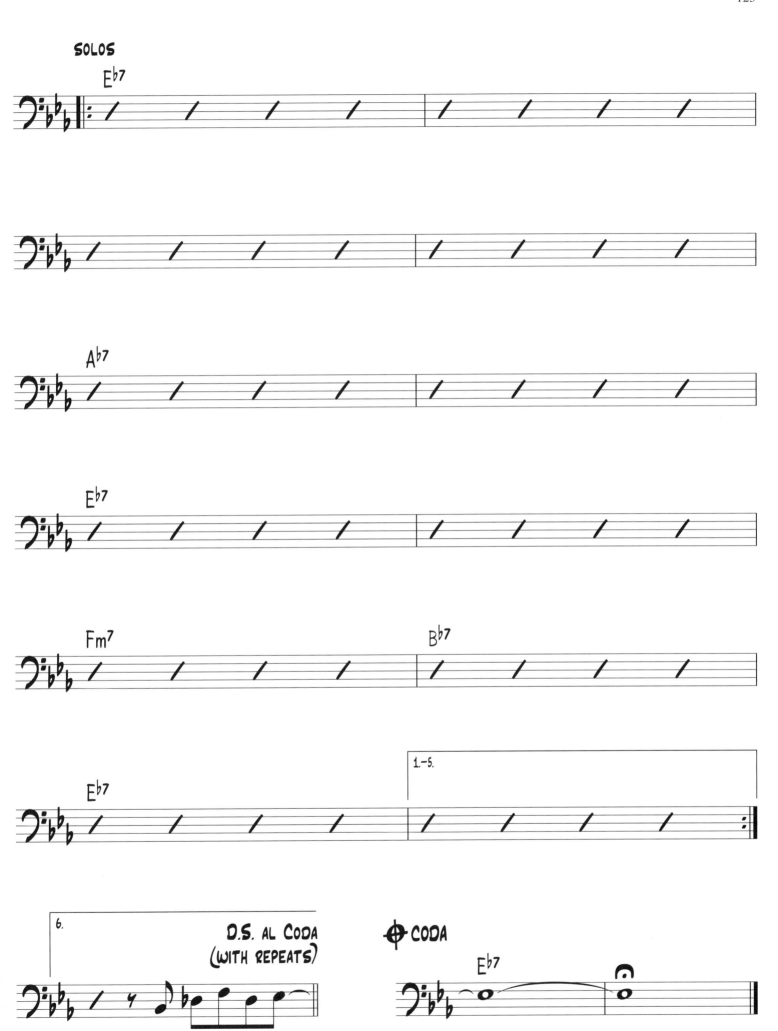

Blues in the Closet

: C Version

By Oscar Pettiford

Cousin Mary

By John Coltrane

𝄢 C Version

SOLOS

$A^{\flat}7$

$D^{\flat}7$

$A^{\flat}7$

D^{7} $D^{\flat}7$

$A^{\flat}7$

1.–5.   6.

D.C. AL CODA (WITH REPEAT)

Every Day I Have the Blues

WORDS AND MUSIC BY
PETER CHATMAN

C Version

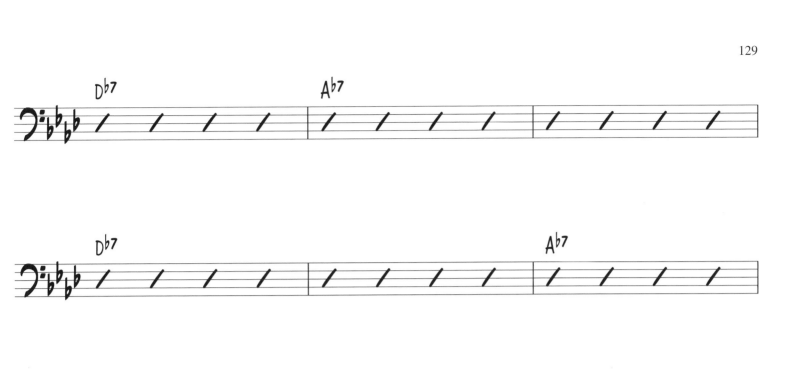

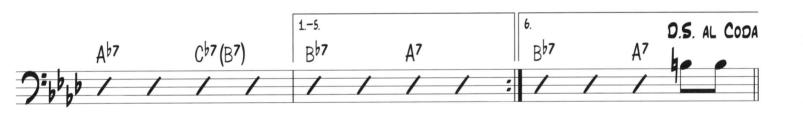

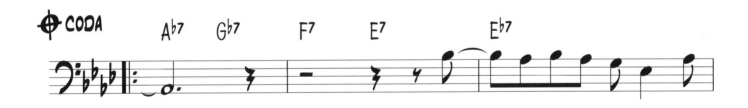

Nostalgia in Times Square

𝄢 C Version

By Charles Mingus

Now See How You Are

𝄢 C Version

BY OSCAR PETTIFORD
AND WOODY HARRIS

NOW'S THE TIME

C VERSION

BY CHARLIE PARKER

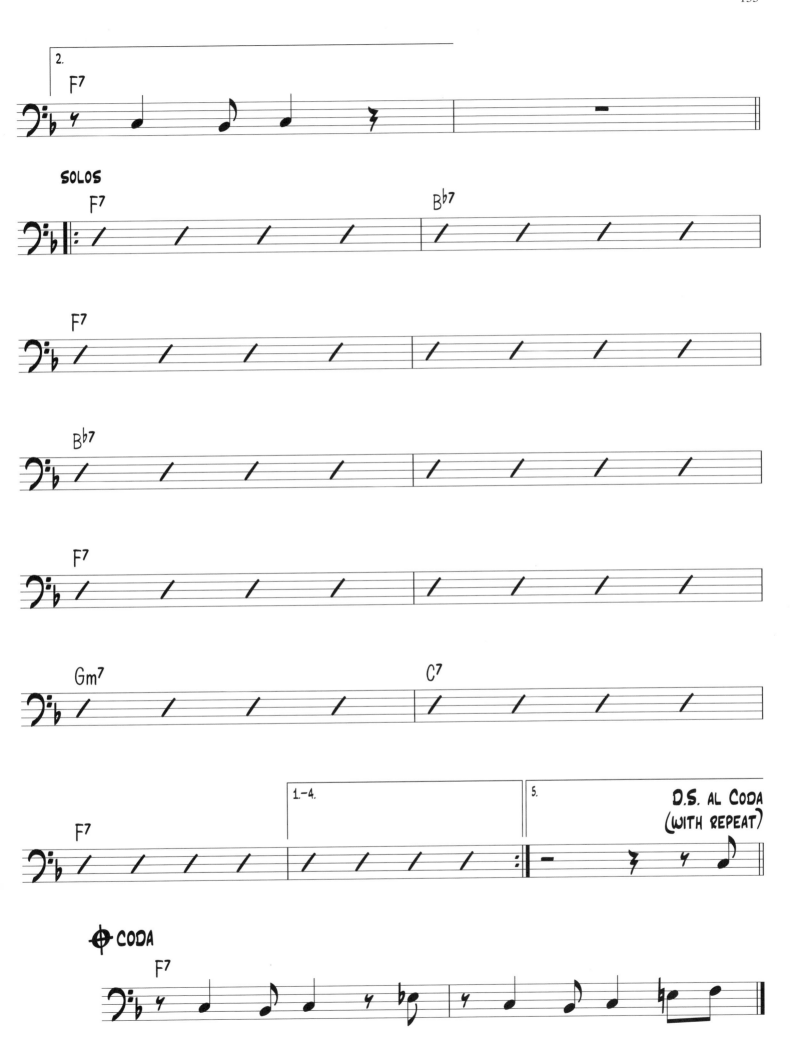

THE SERMON

C VERSION

BY HAMPTON HAWES

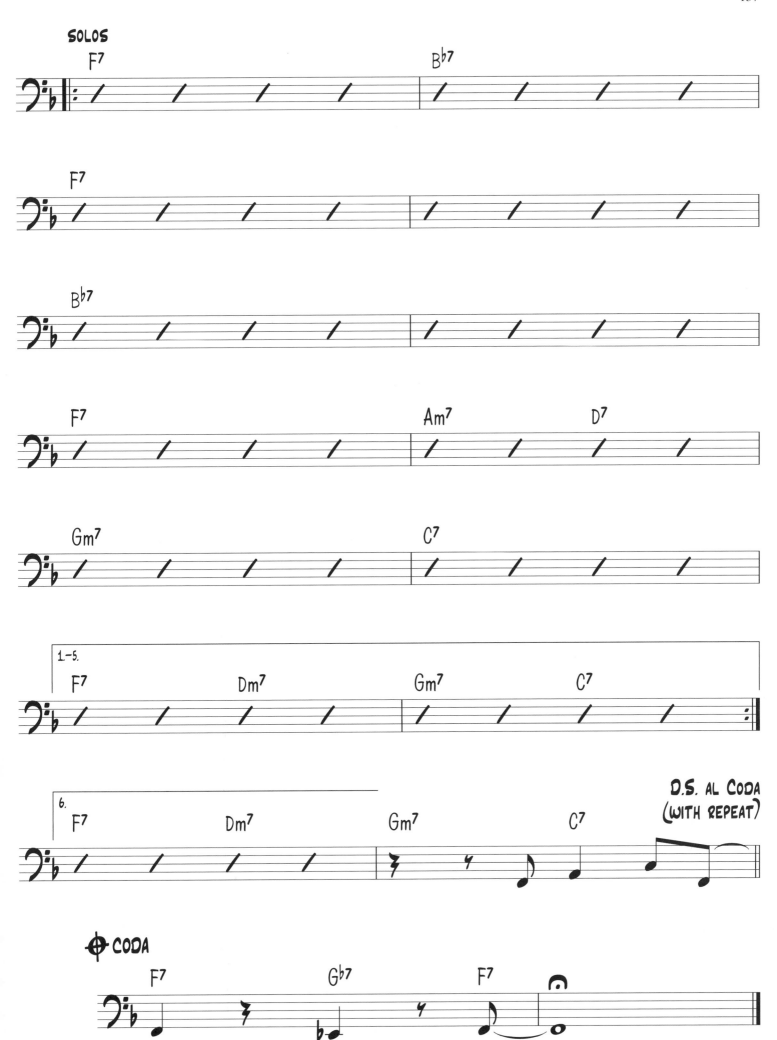

Sonnymoon for Two

C Version

By Sonny Rollins

TENOR MADNESS

C VERSION

BY SONNY ROLLINS

Things Ain't What They Used to Be

C Version

By Mercer Ellington

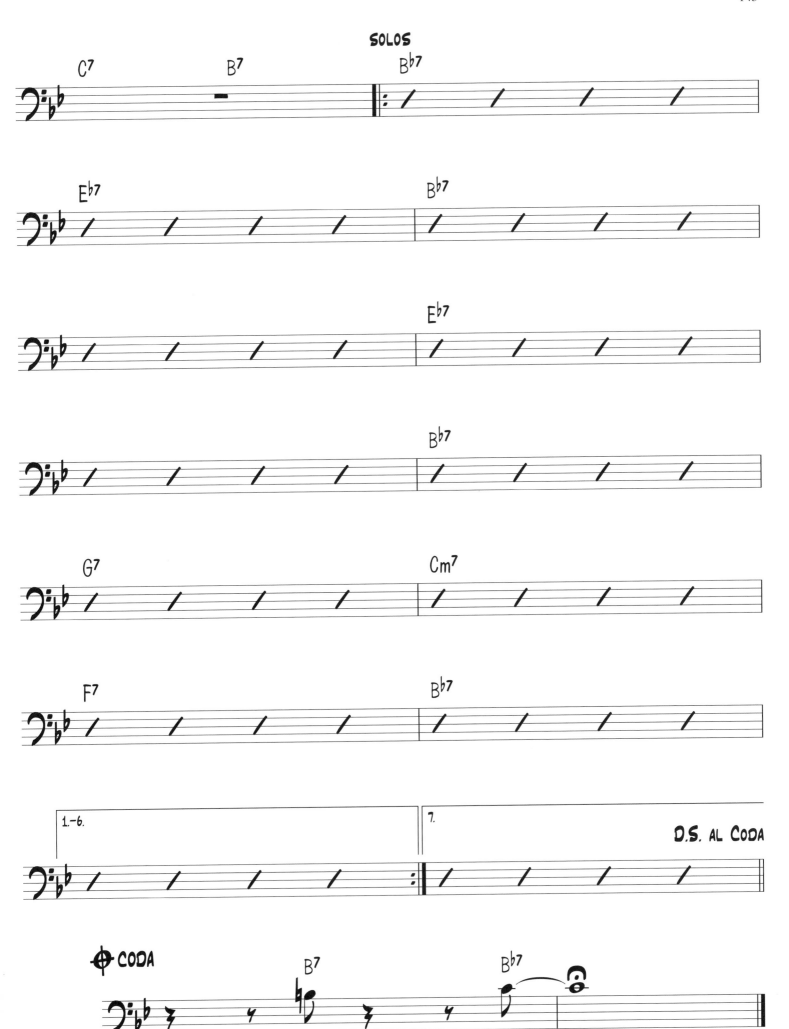

Turnaround

𝄢 C Version

BY ORNETTE COLEMAN

Two Degrees East, Three Degrees West

𝄢 C Version

By John Lewis

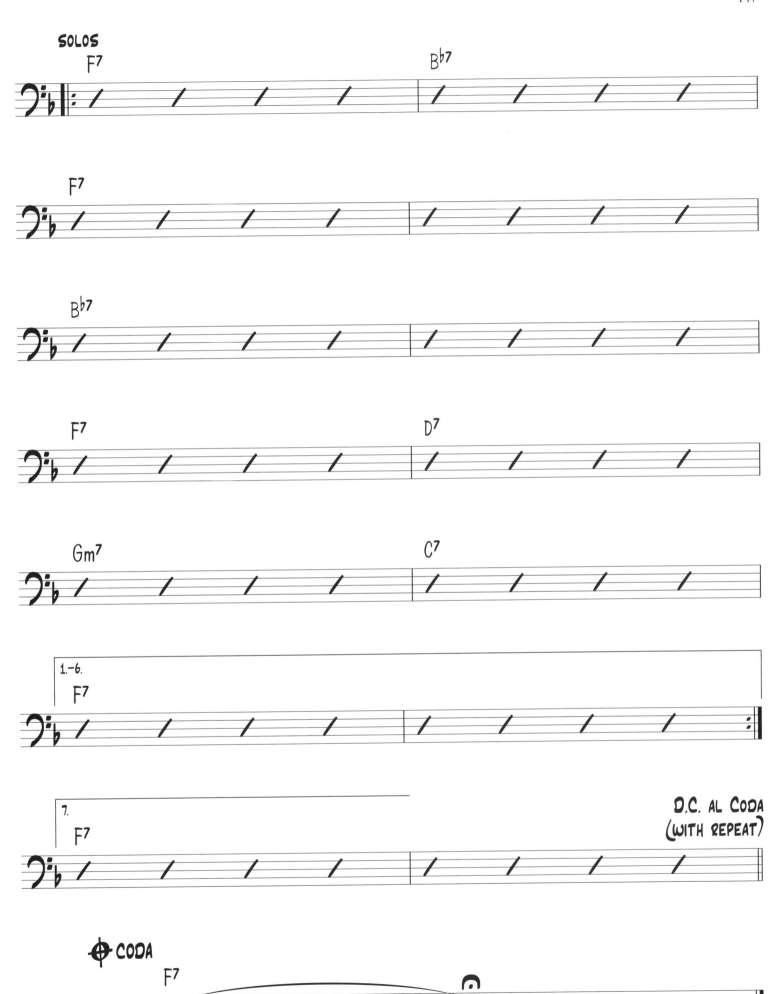

FREDDIE FREELOADER

9: C VERSION

BY MILES DAVIS

IMPROVISING IS EASIER THAN EVER

with this new series for beginning jazz musicians. The Hal Leonard Easy Jazz Play-Along Series includes songs with accessible chord changes and features recordings with novice-friendly tempos. Just follow the streamlined lead sheets in the book and play along with the professionally recorded backing tracks on the CD. The bass or piano can also be removed by turning down the volume on the left or right channel. The audio CD is playable on any CD player. For PC and Mac computer users, the CD is enhanced so you can adjust the recording to any tempo without changing pitch!

1. FIRST JAZZ SONGS
Book/CD Pack

All of Me • All the Things You Are • Autumn Leaves • C-Jam Blues • Comin' Home Baby • Footprints • The Girl from Ipanema (Garôta De Ipanema) • Killer Joe • Little Sunflower • Milestones • Mr. P.C. • On Green Dolphin Street • One for Daddy-O • Reunion Blues • Satin Doll • There Will Never Be Another You • Tune Up • Watermelon Man.
00843225 B♭, E♭, C & Bass Clef Instruments............... $19.99

2. STANDARDS FOR STARTERS
Book/CD Pack

Don't Get Around Much Anymore • Exactly like You • Fly Me to the Moon (In Other Words) • Have You Met Miss Jones? • Honeysuckle Rose • I Remember You • If I Should Lose You • It Could Happen to You • Moon River • My Favorite Things • On a Slow Boat to China • Out of Nowhere • Softly As in a Morning Sunrise • Speak Low • The Very Thought of You • Watch What Happens • The Way You Look Tonight • Yesterdays.
00843226 B♭, E♭, C & Bass Clef Instruments............... $19.99

3. VITAL JAZZ CLASSICS
Book/CD Pack

Afternoon in Paris • Doxy • 500 Miles High • Girl Talk • Holy Land • Impressions • In Walked Bud • The Jive Samba • Lady Bird • Maiden Voyage • Mercy, Mercy, Mercy • My Little Suede Shoes • Record-a-Me • St. Thomas • Solar • Song for My Father • Stolen Moments • Sunny.
00843227 B♭, E♭, C & Bass Clef Instruments............... $19.99

4. BASIC BLUES
Book/CD Pack

All Blues • Birk's Works • Bloomdido • Blue Seven • Blue Train (Blue Trane) • Blues in the Closet • Cousin Mary • Freddie Freeloader • The Jody Grind • Jumpin' with Symphony Sid • Nostalgia in Times Square • Now See How You Are • Now's the Time • Sonnymoon for Two • Tenor Madness • Things Ain't What They Used to Be • Turnaround • Two Degrees East, Three Degrees West.
00843228 B♭, E♭, C & Bass Clef Instruments............... $19.99

7777 W. BLUEMOUND RD. P.O. BOX 13819 MILWAUKEE, WI 53213

Prices, content, and availability subject to change without notice.

Presenting the Hal Leonard JAZZ PLAY-ALONG SERIES

For use with all B-flat, E-flat, Bass Clef and C instruments, the Jazz Play-Along® Series is the ultimate learning tool for all jazz musicians. With musician-friendly lead sheets, melody cues, and other split-track choices on the included CD, these first-of-a-kind packages help you master improvisation while playing some of the greatest tunes of all time. FOR STUDY, each tune includes a split track with: melody cue with proper style and inflection • professional rhythm tracks • choruses for soloing • removable bass part • removable piano part. FOR PERFORMANCE, each tune also has: an additional full stereo accompaniment track (no melody) • additional choruses for soloing.

1. DUKE ELLINGTON
00841644 ....$16.95

1A. MAIDEN VOYAGE/ALL BLUES
00843158 ....$15.99

2. MILES DAVIS
00841645 ....$16.95

3. THE BLUES
00841646 ....$16.99

4. JAZZ BALLADS
00841691 ....$16.99

5. BEST OF BEBOP
00841689 ....$16.95

6. JAZZ CLASSICS WITH EASY CHANGES
00841690 ....$16.99

7. ESSENTIAL JAZZ STANDARDS
00843000 ....$16.99

8. ANTONIO CARLOS JOBIM AND THE ART OF THE BOSSA NOVA
00843001 ....$16.95

9. DIZZY GILLESPIE
00843002 ....$16.99

10. DISNEY CLASSICS
00843003 ....$16.99

11. RODGERS AND HART FAVORITES
00843004 ....$16.99

12. ESSENTIAL JAZZ CLASSICS
00843005 ....$16.99

13. JOHN COLTRANE
00843006 ....$16.95

14. IRVING BERLIN
00843007 ....$15.99

15. RODGERS & HAMMERSTEIN
00843008 ....$15.99

16. COLE PORTER
00843009 ....$15.95

17. COUNT BASIE
00843010 ....$16.95

18. HAROLD ARLEN
00843011 ....$15.95

19. COOL JAZZ
00843012 ....$15.95

20. CHRISTMAS CAROLS
00843080 ....$14.95

21. RODGERS AND HART CLASSICS
00843014 ....$14.95

22. WAYNE SHORTER
00843015 ....$16.95

23. LATIN JAZZ
00843016 ....$16.95

24. EARLY JAZZ STANDARDS
00843017 ....$14.95

25. CHRISTMAS JAZZ
00843018 ....$16.95

26. CHARLIE PARKER
00843019 ....$16.95

27. GREAT JAZZ STANDARDS
00843020 ....$16.99

28. BIG BAND ERA
00843021 ....$15.99

29. LENNON AND MCCARTNEY
00843022 ....$16.95

30. BLUES' BEST
00843023 ....$15.99

31. JAZZ IN THREE
00843024 ....$15.99

32. BEST OF SWING
00843025 ....$15.99

33. SONNY ROLLINS
00843029 ....$15.95

34. ALL TIME STANDARDS
00843030 ....$15.99

35. BLUESY JAZZ
00843031 ....$16.99

36. HORACE SILVER
00843032 ....$16.99

37. BILL EVANS
00843033 ....$16.95

38. YULETIDE JAZZ
00843034 ....$16.95

39. "ALL THE THINGS YOU ARE" & MORE JEROME KERN SONGS
00843035 ....$15.99

40. BOSSA NOVA
00843036 ....$15.99

41. CLASSIC DUKE ELLINGTON
00843037 ....$16.99

42. GERRY MULLIGAN FAVORITES
00843038 ....$16.99

43. GERRY MULLIGAN CLASSICS
00843039 ....$16.95

44. OLIVER NELSON
00843040 ....$16.95

45. JAZZ AT THE MOVIES
00843041 ....$15.99

46. BROADWAY JAZZ STANDARDS
00843042 ....$15.99

47. CLASSIC JAZZ BALLADS
00843043 ....$15.99

48. BEBOP CLASSICS
00843044 ....$16.99

49. MILES DAVIS STANDARDS
00843045 ....$16.95

50. GREAT JAZZ CLASSICS
00843046 ....$15.99

51. UP-TEMPO JAZZ
00843047 ....$15.99

52. STEVIE WONDER
00843048 ....$16.99

53. RHYTHM CHANGES
00843049 ....$15.99

54. "MOONLIGHT IN VERMONT" AND OTHER GREAT STANDARDS
00843050 ....$15.99

55. BENNY GOLSON
00843052 ....$15.95

56. "GEORGIA ON MY MIND" & OTHER SONGS BY HOAGY CARMICHAEL
00843056 ....$15.99

57. VINCE GUARALDI
00843057 ....$16.99

58. MORE LENNON AND MCCARTNEY
00843059 ....$15.99

59. SOUL JAZZ
00843060 ....$15.99

60. DEXTER GORDON
00843061 ....$15.95

61. MONGO SANTAMARIA
00843062 ....$15.95

62. JAZZ-ROCK FUSION
00843063 ....$16.99

63. CLASSICAL JAZZ
00843064.................................$14.95

64. TV TUNES
00843065.................................$14.95

65. SMOOTH JAZZ
00843066.................................$16.99

66. A CHARLIE BROWN CHRISTMAS
00843067.................................$16.99

67. CHICK COREA
00843068.................................$15.95

68. CHARLES MINGUS
00843069.................................$16.95

69. CLASSIC JAZZ
00843071.................................$15.99

70. THE DOORS
00843072.................................$14.95

71. COLE PORTER CLASSICS
00843073.................................$14.95

72. CLASSIC JAZZ BALLADS
00843074.................................$15.99

73. JAZZ/BLUES
00843075.................................$14.95

74. BEST JAZZ CLASSICS
00843076.................................$15.99

75. PAUL DESMOND
00843077.................................$14.95

76. BROADWAY JAZZ BALLADS
00843078.................................$15.99

77. JAZZ ON BROADWAY
00843079.................................$15.99

78. STEELY DAN
00843070.................................$14.99

79. MILES DAVIS CLASSICS
00843081.................................$15.99

80. JIMI HENDRIX
00843083.................................$15.99

81. FRANK SINATRA – CLASSICS
00843084.................................$15.99

82. FRANK SINATRA – STANDARDS
00843085.................................$15.99

83. ANDREW LLOYD WEBBER
00843104.................................$14.95

84. BOSSA NOVA CLASSICS
00843105.................................$14.95

85. MOTOWN HITS
00843109.................................$14.95

86. BENNY GOODMAN
00843110.................................$14.95

87. DIXIELAND
00843111.................................$14.95

88. DUKE ELLINGTON FAVORITES
00843112.................................$14.95

89. IRVING BERLIN FAVORITES
00843113.................................$14.95

90. THELONIOUS MONK CLASSICS
00841262.................................$16.99

91.THELONIOUS MONK FAVORITES
00841263.................................$16.99

92. LEONARD BERNSTEIN
00450134.................................$15.99

93. DISNEY FAVORITES
00843142.................................$14.99

94. RAY
00843143.................................$14.99

95. JAZZ AT THE LOUNGE
00843144.................................V$14.99

96. LATIN JAZZ STANDARDS
00843145.................................$14.99

97. MAYBE I'M AMAZED★
00843148.................................$15.99

98. DAVE FRISHBERG
00843149.................................$15.99

99. SWINGING STANDARDS
00843150.................................$14.99

100. LOUIS ARMSTRONG
00740423.................................$15.99

101. BUD POWELL
00843152.................................$14.99

102. JAZZ POP
00843153.................................$14.99

**103. ON GREEN DOLPHIN STREET
& OTHER JAZZ CLASSICS**
00843154.................................$14.99

104. ELTON JOHN
00843155.................................$14.99

105. SOULFUL JAZZ
00843151.................................$15.99

106. SLO' JAZZ
00843117.................................$14.99

107. MOTOWN CLASSICS
00843116.................................$14.99

108. JAZZ WALTZ
00843159.................................$15.99

109. OSCAR PETERSON
00843160.................................$16.99

110. JUST STANDARDS
00843161.................................$15.99

111. COOL CHRISTMAS
00843162.................................$15.99

112. PAQUITO D'RIVERA – LATIN JAZZ★
48020662.................................$16.99

113. PAQUITO D'RIVERA – BRAZILIAN JAZZ★
48020663.................................$19.99

114. MODERN JAZZ QUARTET FAVORITES
00843163.................................$15.99

115. THE SOUND OF MUSIC
00843164.................................$15.99

116. JACO PASTORIUS
00843165.................................$15.99

117. ANTONIO CARLOS JOBIM – MORE HITS
00843166.................................$15.99

118. BIG JAZZ STANDARDS COLLECTION
00843167.................................$27.50

119. JELLY ROLL MORTON
00843168.................................$15.99

120. J.S. BACH
00843169.................................$15.99

121. DJANGO REINHARDT
00843170.................................$15.99

122. PAUL SIMON
00843182.................................$16.99

123. BACHARACH & DAVID
00843185.................................$15.99

124. JAZZ-ROCK HORN HITS
00843186.................................$15.99

126. COUNT BASIE CLASSICS
00843157.................................$15.99

127. CHUCK MANGIONE
00843188.................................$15.99

132. STAN GETZ ESSENTIALS
00843193.................................$15.99

133. STAN GETZ FAVORITES
00843194.................................$15.99

134. NURSERY RHYMES★
00843196.................................$17.99

135. JEFF BECK
00843197.................................$15.99

136. NAT ADDERLEY
00843198.................................$15.99

137. WES MONTGOMERY
00843199.................................$15.99

138. FREDDIE HUBBARD
00843200.................................$15.99

139. JULIAN "CANNONBALL" ADDERLEY
00843201.................................$15.99

141. BILL EVANS STANDARDS
00843156.................................$15.99

150. JAZZ IMPROV BASICS
00843195.................................$19.99

151. MODERN JAZZ QUARTET CLASSICS
00843209.................................$15.99

157. HYMNS
00843217.................................$15.99

162. BIG CHRISTMAS COLLECTION
00843221.................................$24.99

★These CDs do not include split tracks.

Hal•Leonard BLUES PLAY-ALONG

For use with all the C, B♭, Bass Clef and E♭ Instruments, the Hal Leonard Blues Play-Along Series is the ultimate jamming tool for all blues musicians.

With easy-to-read lead sheets, and other split-track choices on the included CD, these first-of-a-kind packages will bring your local blues jam right into your house! Each song on the CD includes two tracks: a full stereo mix, and a split track mix with removable guitar, bass, piano, and harp parts. The CD is playable on any CD player, and is also enhanced so Mac and PC users can adjust the recording to any tempo without changing the pitch!

1. Chicago Blues
All Your Love (I Miss Loving) • Easy Baby • I Ain't Got You • I'm Your Hoochie Coochie Man • Killing Floor • Mary Had a Little Lamb • Messin' with the Kid • Sweet Home Chicago.
00843106 Book/CD Pack $12.99

2. Texas Blues
Hide Away • If You Love Me Like You Say • Mojo Hand • Okie Dokie Stomp • Pride and Joy • Reconsider Baby • T-Bone Shuffle • The Things That I Used to Do.
00843107 Book/CD Pack $12.99

3. Slow Blues
Don't Throw Your Love on Me So Strong • Five Long Years • I Can't Quit You Baby • I Just Want to Make Love to You • The Sky Is Crying • (They Call It) Stormy Monday (Stormy Monday Blues) • Sweet Little Angel • Texas Flood.
00843108 Book/CD Pack $12.99

4. Shuffle Blues
Beautician Blues • Bright Lights, Big City • Further on up the Road • I'm Tore Down • Juke • Let Me Love You Baby • Look at Little Sister • Rock Me Baby.
00843171 Book/CD Pack $12.99

5. B.B. King
Everyday I Have the Blues • It's My Own Fault Darlin' • Just Like a Woman • Please Accept My Love • Sweet Sixteen • The Thrill Is Gone • Why I Sing the Blues • You Upset Me Baby.
00843172 Book/CD Pack $14.99

6. Jazz Blues
Birk's Works • Blues in the Closet • Cousin Mary • Freddie Freeloader • Now's the Time • Tenor Madness • Things Ain't What They Used to Be • Turnaround.
00843175 Book/CD Pack $12.99

7. Howlin' Wolf
Built for Comfort • Forty-Four • How Many More Years • Killing Floor • Moanin' at Midnight • Shake for Me • Sitting on Top of the World • Smokestack Lightning.
00843176 Book/CD Pack $12.99

8. Blues Classics
Baby, Please Don't Go • Boom Boom • Born Under a Bad Sign • Dust My Broom • How Long, How Long Blues • I Ain't Superstitious • It Hurts Me Too • My Babe.
00843177 Book/CD Pack $12.99

9. Albert Collins
Brick • Collins' Mix • Don't Lose Your Cool • Frost Bite • Frosty • I Ain't Drunk • Master Charge • Trash Talkin'.
00843178 Book/CD Pack $12.99

10. Uptempo Blues
Cross Road Blues (Crossroads) • Give Me Back My Wig • Got My Mo Jo Working • The House Is Rockin' • Paying the Cost to Be the Boss • Rollin' and Tumblin' • Turn on Your Love Light • You Can't Judge a Book by the Cover.
00843179 Book/CD Pack $12.99

11. Christmas Blues
Back Door Santa • Blue Christmas • Dig That Crazy Santa Claus • Merry Christmas, Baby • Please Come Home for Christmas • Santa Baby • Soulful Christmas.
00843203 Book/CD Pack $12.99

12. Jimmy Reed
Ain't That Lovin' You Baby • Baby, What You Want Me to Do • Big Boss Man • Bright Lights, Big City • Going to New York • Honest I Do • You Don't Have to Go • You Got Me Dizzy.
00843204 Book/CD Pack $12.99

FOR MORE INFORMATION, SEE YOUR LOCAL MUSIC DEALER, OR WRITE TO:

HAL•LEONARD® CORPORATION
7777 W. BLUEMOUND RD. P.O. BOX 13819 MILWAUKEE, WI 53213